The Race of my Life

50 essays on living with cancer

Written by: **Dr. David C. Eitrheim, M.D. and
Amy J. Eitrheim**

Foreword by: **Norman D. Eitrheim**

The Race of my Life
©2016 by David and Amy Eitrheim

ISBN: 978-1519133458

Table of contents

Foreword

The motivation to write was to inform patients, friends and family through weekly journaling in his CaringBridge site of his experiences, feelings and reminiscences. His aggressive cancer had been treated with both chemo and radiation therapy and the side effects had been severe, but he had been able to return to his work as a family practice doctor for a few months. Now the cancer had returned with a fury, and he was told that he had six to nine months to live. It was that prognosis from the Mayo Clinic in Rochester that prompted him to write each week in CaringBridge. Some chapters were written in the middle of the night when he couldn't sleep because of chemo side effects. The motivation to write was to share his thoughts as a dying man accepting death and living with cancer rather than dying from cancer.

There never was any intention by Dr. David Eitrheim to write a book. Readers of his CaringBridge entries suggested that his journal be compiled into a book. Over 60,000 "hits" on his site were evidence that many found his writings not only interesting but helpful. He was convinced that a book could be helpful to his patients and others who walk through hard times.

When I, his father, learned of the return of the cancer, I found it difficult to accept. I could not understand why a needed, competent, and caring doctor who loved his work and his patients should be struck down at the age of 57. Why would someone who hasn't smoked or chewed be attacked by cancer of the tongue? It wasn't fair; it wasn't just; it wasn't understandable. As I read his journaling, my son became my mentor. He guided me, his pastor father, into deeper realms of faith, grace, acceptance, gratitude, spirituality and joy.

Walter Mondale, speaking at Hubert Humphrey's funeral said, "He taught us how to live and he taught us how to die." Dave's journal entries are about both living and dying. Here are few excerpts:

FAITH –"As Amy and I prepare for the end of this earthly life, I am assured of a much greater life in Christ after death. It is with confidence that we can say that while we may have many things to think about, we have nothing to worry about."

GRATITUDE - "I will leave this life without regrets. Instead I thank God for having blessed me with a life that few on earth will ever have."

VOCATION – "I have been so richly blessed by the privilege of entering into my patient' lives…. After 27 years of practice in Menomonie, my patients have become my friends. My care for them has been more than just a moral obligation, it is a desire to help friends and their families have a better life."

HOPE – "My cancer will continue to require pain control. The Great Healer's last great act of healing in my life will be death, when pain and cancer no longer occupy my mind or body. At that time, God shows what final healing is in store for us."

JOY - "When we get to the point where enjoying the success of others is more important than our own success, we find our greatest joy."

OPPORTUNITY – "As we prepare for my death, the process of dying has instead created a new opportunity to share God's spirit and be recipients of God's grace through the kindness of others."

ACCEPTANCE – "I have already had conversation with Amy and our sons about my wishes at the end of life. I want to be comfortable and I don't want life unnecessarily extended. God can call me home when it is time. At life's end, I won't be trying one last futile therapy to extend that time by a few days or weeks."

HEALING – "We should give thanks to God for all of the healing that we take for granted but is no less miraculous….It is time for us to redefine miracles…Just because we have scientific advancements that explain more of the world around us, we should never lose our sense of awe in the supernatural. Our entire world and life is one big supernatural miracle."

I have been helped by Dave's reflections on life and death during his journey of living with cancer. Hopefully, readers will also be blessed by this book.

Bishop Emeritus Norman Eitrheim

Introduction

I worked for twenty-seven years as a family physician in the small town of Menomonie, Wisconsin. While my days were filled with the mental challenges of medicine, my favorite past-time challenged me both physically and mentally: running. I ran cross-country in high school as a teenager, and my first marathon in 1976. I ran it in high-top canvas sneakers, as specialized running shoes hadn't been invented yet. Over the years, the distance of my races increased, from 26.2 miles, to 100. I was cruising through life pretty smoothly, until my world was turned upside-down by a cancer diagnosis.

There are many parallels between training for, and running a marathon or an ultramarathon, and living through the struggles of cancer and the many side effects of its treatments.

One-hundred-mile races, in particular, are filled with highs and lows. You learn how to get through the lows: slow down the pace; take in more calories and liquids. The most difficult time in a race occurs in the middle of the night. After running eighty to ninety miles my eyelids feel like they are loaded with heavy bags of sand. I find myself wishing I could take a nap. Most helpful, though, may be the encouraging words from crew members and volunteers at aid stations, or a fellow runner who runs side-by-side with you. You learn to look for and appreciate the highs as well: running through beautiful scenery; meeting new friends and spending quality time with old; the feeling of great accomplishment at finishing the race you set out to run; the thrill of persevering through difficult circumstances.

Running a hard race and living with cancer can both involve pain. I was surprised to find that when the side effects of chemo were at their worst, it felt similar to the feelings I got in the middle of the night in a long race: nausea, vomiting, blisters, extreme fatigue, and psychological anguish, to name a few.

In running, and completing, in ultra-marathons, I learned that listening to my body was necessary to be successful. I found that my body would tell me what to eat by craving certain foods at different times. During a race, I couldn't eat enough carbs; after the race, I craved fatty foods. My running buddies and I established a great tradition of seeking out the nearest pub for a delicious cheese burger after the race.

I began treatment for my cancer, and starting posting on CaringBridge as a means to communicate my experiences and reflections about life, death, faith, and hope. It also became an avenue by which I could keep in contact with family and friends, and let them know how I was doing. I had thought that I would be alive, and be able to write, for only a short time, given the seriousness of my cancer. But, to everyone's surprise and delight, I survived far longer than anyone expected. These entries, originally posted in CaringBridge nearly weekly for a year, are the chapters in this book.

A chronology of some of the events for the past few years is found at the end of this book.

I would like to acknowledge the help of my wife, Amy in suggesting ideas for, and editing, my CaringBridge entries. She cheerfully offered to 'fix' my writings each week, and I wisely accepted. Our sons supplied much-needed computer support and help in transitioning this into a publishable format. Also, my aunt Joan Eitrheim assisted with major editing for the final copy of this compilation of essays. She is a retired English teacher, and I appreciated her input so much. Thanks to my dad for writing the Foreword, and for encouraging me to publish this in book form. Finally, many thanks to friend and artist Matthew Wigdahl for creating the original artwork for the book cover.

Unpublished entries, as well as photos, can be viewed online at the original site:

http://www.caringbridge.org/visit/daveeitrheim

Dave Eitrheim
December 7, 2015

Dave's Story

Welcome to our CaringBridge site. We've created it to keep friends and family updated. We appreciate your support and words of hope and encouragement during this time when it matters most.

I was diagnosed with squamous cell carcinoma of the tongue at the Mayo clinic in Rochester, MN, July 22 2013. The cancer was resected, along with lymph nodes and salivary glands, the next day. Unfortunately, two lymph nodes came back positive for cancer. It was classified as a stage IVa (aggressive in nature.)

I started chemo and radiation therapy in early September. Since I was a healthy and active non-smoker, the negative side effects were severe. The mouth sores made it too difficult to eat, or even to talk. I ended up with a feeding tube into my stomach, which we used for about six weeks. The pain and the fatigue were difficult to manage. But I was feeling well enough in December to enjoy a vacation with Amy, Nathan and Eric, and their girlfriends, in Texas and Florida.

I returned to work in January, grateful to be back working with my terrific nurses and colleagues, and seeing my patients. I had received so many cards while I was gone, and felt truly blessed to have had all the support.

A return appointment with my surgeon, and oncologist, and a PET scan in mid-February was scheduled. Everything checked out normal: there was no evidence of cancer! We were able to enjoy a week of skiing in Colorado with such reassuring news.

As the spring progressed, however, the pain, now spreading to the left (contra-lateral to the cancer) side, increased. Sleep was sporadic, with the pain becoming increasingly difficult to control. I was taking more and more narcotics in the evening, and the work days were becoming hard to get through.

A repeat head/neck CT and MRI were performed in early April, and still did not show any cancer. It did show an enlarging sublingual salivary gland. I had that taken out on May 5th, with the hope of decreasing pain. That, too, was tested, and had no cancer in it.

When the surgical (intra-oral) site failed to heal, more tests were done. This time, on May 22, the PET revealed the cancer had spread to lymph nodes on the left side of my neck, and there was a spot in the chest. Skin nodules were biopsied, and also showed metastatic cancer. We were told it was terminal, and that the cancer was growing rapidly.

Since that time, we have visited with the palliative (pain control) physician and developed a pain management regimen. We will be inviting hospice into our home when the time is right, to assist me in my final days.

One of the most distressing parts of being diagnosed with recurring cancer was the abrupt and unexpected end to my work career. My hope would be that this website could be an avenue by which I could connect with patients, family, and friends, even if only electronically,

We welcome your prayers, support, and visits. Our door is open.

As Amy and I prepare for the end of this earthly life, I am assured of a much greater life in Christ after death. It is with confidence that we can say, that, while we may have many things to think about, we have nothing to worry about.

Peace be with you.

Dave and Amy

1. A blessed life

June 3, 2014

I am thankful for having lived a privileged life.

It began by growing up in a loving, caring family in the United States. Although many of us may wish for change in our country, you don't need to travel through many other nations in this world to realize the magnitude of our fortune to be born in the US and grow up one of its citizens. My parents are in their mid-80's and are truly exceptional people. Growing up in that family provided a great foundation for a life of service and care for others.

I've enjoyed thirty-one years of a loving marriage to Amy. It has been a great partnership. I have so much appreciated her generous care of our sons and others, and particularly of me as I have gone through the diagnosis and treatment of cancer. Facing a terminal illness like cancer is not a task that anyone should have to undertake alone. Our two sons are grown up. We are proud of the men they have become and what they have accomplished. I have been fortunate to live through the time when our sons were under roof and growing up. When you know that you are leaving this earth at the end of life, you realize that your offspring are your pride and joy, and an extension of your life on earth.

As a family physician, I have been privileged to be invited into the lives of others: to be the first to see their newborn baby, to comfort a grieving family at death, or to care for someone going through a hospitalization or major illness. These are among the most important events in life, and I have been so richly blessed by the privilege of entering into my patients' lives during those critical events. After twenty seven years of practice in Menomonie Wisconsin, my patients have become my friends. My care for them has been more than just a moral obligation; it is a desire to help friends and their families have a better life.

On the first day of work in 1987, I was paired with Barb Biesterveld, R.N., who has been an indispensable team member; Jackie Weber joined us seven years ago when our practice expanded. They have been a God-send in a busy medical practice. They have always cared deeply for our patients. The abrupt and unexpected end to my career on April 30 2014 left no time for closure with patients and colleagues. I am grateful for the opportunity that CaringBridge provides for connecting with all of you.

I will leave this life without regrets. Instead I thank God for having blessed me with a life that few on earth will ever have.

Thanks be to God.

***

In what ways do you believe you have lived a blessed or privileged life?

Would you trade your life for someone else's whose life you envy?

2. An African lesson in prayer and healing

June 10, 2014

I was reminded recently of one of the many life lessons that I learned in Cameroon, Africa. After finishing family medicine residency twenty eight years ago, my wife Amy and I spent five months working at a medical mission station of the American Lutheran Church in Cameroon.

The very first patient that I saw was an eleven year old Cameroonian girl who had a traumatic compound fracture of the femur (thighbone). For the past two weeks, she and her parents had awaited my arrival, while an African witch doctor packed mud into the open wound (standard treatment). I performed surgery to open the girl's thigh and remove all of the dead bone and infected flesh, leaving a large open wound to allow the infection to drain and slowly heal. It was a surgery that took me beyond my training and experience, but needed to be done in order to save her life.

But before starting the surgery the African nurse who assisted me asked me to pray. I asked God to help heal the girl. The African nurse interpreted it into the girl's native language; he then also added his own prayer.

In the weeks that followed, after performing several surgeries together, with the nurse adding on his own prayer at the end of mine, I asked him what he was saying. He replied that my prayers asked God to help heal the patient. He needed to clarify my prayer, telling the African patients that God is the healer and. that it is the doctor and nurse who are merely helpers. Apparently my weak American prayer that asked God to help heal instead of acknowledging that God is the Great Healer wasn't going to be sufficient as a stand- alone pre-operative prayer.

My prayer had not given full credit to God for the healing that occurs. After I changed my subsequent pre-operative prayers to truly acknowledge God as the Healer, the African nurse quit adding on to my prayers.

I performed two more surgeries in the next several weeks on the girl as we struggled to control the infected leg and bone with dressing changes, drains, and IV antibiotics. Before the third surgery, I was ready to discuss with the parents that amputation might be the only way to save her life.

When I talked with the family, the African nurse had just finished an initial conversation with the parents. The parents asked if there was any hope that the leg could be saved. The nurse quickly responded that "with God all things are possible and God will continue to heal." After that, I really couldn't start the conversation about amputation and fortunately never needed to.

With many prayers she continued to heal. Four and a half months after our first operation, her wound had finally closed, and she had just started walking. Her parents announced to me that they wanted to take her home the next morning. I offered to have one of the missionaries drive her to their village in a car. The father replied that a car wasn't necessary since their village was "only nine miles away."

The next day they left at sunrise, and with the assistance of mother, father, and other family members, they made it half way home. At noon, a large number of neighbors met them on the road. They fed the family lunch and then carried the eleven year old Cameroonian girl the rest of the way back to their village.

Since the days when my weak American prayer needed correction by an African nurse, I have never lost sight of the power of the Great Healer to heal. I have realized that as a physician in the United States, I am given far too much credit for healing. Indeed, our body's capacity to heal and resist disease is amazing evidence of the power of God.

I took my second round of chemotherapy today, in the hopes of reducing pain and swelling in my jaw and neck. The small relief in pain after the first round of chemotherapy was noticeable and much appreciated. Meanwhile, the Great Healer stands by with comfort for me, our family, and the many people who struggle with issues of chronic pain or disease.

It is a time of my life where I appreciate the days where pain and fatigue don't rule the day. My cancer will continue to require pain control. The Great Healer's last great act of healing in my life will be death, when pain and cancer no longer occupy my mind or body. At that time, God shows what final healing is in store for us.

***

How much credit do we give God for healing?

Do you believe either of these statements: "Everything is life is a miracle?" or "Nothing in life is a miracle?"

Is out body's ability to heal miraculous or simply expected based on the science of biology?

3. Another African lesson: The value of community

June 16, 2014

When Amy and I lived in Cameroon Africa twenty eight years ago, there were many cultural differences that became evident. Day by day we learned how the Mbaya people who lived in Garoua Boulai, Cameroon, thought, lived, and cared for each other in many beautiful ways.

My most memorable surgery was a hysterectomy. I was once again working above my training level. But with no one else available who could possibly perform the operation, I was their only choice for this life-saving procedure. The surgery started well until I reached the most critical part of the operation. I had placed clamps on the large uterine artery, but if the clamp let loose before I could tie it off, the patient would bleed to death.

At that critical moment, the main generator that supplied electricity and lights to the hospital malfunctioned. We were left in total darkness in the windowless operating room. The African nurse assisting me could be heard but not seen. In broken English, he said, "No problem. This happened once before. I be right back."

He left the dark operating room and for several minutes we waited: the African patient lying on the operating table, fully conscious and awake, but numb from the waist down from spinal anesthesia, and I. The nurse soon returned and proudly held up two flashlights at the foot of the operating table. I finished the hysterectomy successfully with my surgical assistant holding the light source.

The most remarkable part of this story is that the Africans never talked about what had happened. If this event had occurred in the United States, there would have been investigations, lawsuits, congressional hearings, and legislators stumbling over each other to author a bill that would assure that this never happened again.

I was stunned that this event was not a big deal. It told me that the Mbaya people are not entitled people. Bad events happen in Africa, and there was no search to blame someone for the power failure. There was no expectation that a surgical procedure would occur flawlessly. They were accepting of misfortune or mistakes as a part of life. They were resourceful and grateful.

The Mbaya people had a strong and caring community. Community was their form of entitlement. I never saw a patient who couldn't pay a hospital bill. It wasn't a government program that stepped up to pay, but rather friends and neighbors and relatives. In fact, the pool of relatives was so large that all cousins or even remotely related people were referred to as brother or sister.

If a Mbaya person asked for food or for something they needed, relatives, friends, and neighbors were quick to supply their need. When we admitted a patient to the hospital, relatives would arrive and sleep under the patient's hospital bed. They cooked meals over an open fire, laundered clothing, and provided care for the hospitalized family member. Although I would see signs of malnourishment, I never saw a Mbaya person starve to death. Relatives and community would never allow that to occur.

In many ways, these last weeks have felt like Amy and I are members of the Mbaya community in Cameroon. After learning that my tongue cancer is now terminal, we have been overwhelmed by your love, support and prayers. Cards, letters, flowers, food, and CaringBridge entries have reminded us of how blessed we are to live in this community. We do not feel entitled to all this attention and are stunned with the outpouring of love.

It will be far easier to leave this world, knowing that my wife Amy, our sons Nathan and Eric, my parents Norm and Clarice, and others dearest to me are surrounded by this community of caring people.

Amy and I are grateful that our community is strong, loving, and giving.

In the meantime, if you are ever having surgery in Menomonie, rest assured that there are backup generators and that no one will need to search for a flashlight to finish your operation.

***

How large and helpful is your community? What stories come to mind of a helpful community?

Would your relative or friends step forward if you needed their financial help or physical care?

Would you step forward in the same way to help family or friends?

4. "What a blow to clean living!"

June 24, 2014

A friend of ours had one comment when she learned about my tongue cancer: "What a blow to clean living!"

It is true that I have been blessed with extremely good health during my lifetime. Yet, eating healthy foods, never smoking or chewing tobacco, and running marathons and ultra-marathons didn't prevent my cancer. I'm not suggesting that you should now reach for a cigarette, shot glass and lounge chair to ward off cancer or any other health misfortune. None of our good health habits comes with a guarantee of good health. My cancer can be used as Exhibit A.

Last Saturday I joined my running friends in our annual pilgrimage to Duluth, MN, where we have run Grandma's Marathon. Grandma's and the Boston Marathon are my two favorite marathons. I like these two because I never race them. I've always run them alongside a friend who has a goal, and I want to help him attain that goal. The camaraderie of training with others and then completing a race together has been the greatest motivator to keep me running, mile after mile and year after year.

I still remember the day that I signed up to run cross country in ninth grade. It was a sad day. I had always played football. But as a late bloomer who was now one of the smallest boys in my class, I had no other choice: cross country was my sport. I was so disappointed.

God does work in "strange and mysterious ways." I never could have fathomed that ninth grade cross country was the start of a life-long treasured pastime that would be a source of great joy and adventures.

My first marathon in 1976 was the City of Lakes Marathon in Minneapolis. There were only 240 runners in that event, and it was the only marathon in Minnesota. I ran it in canvas tennis shoes as "running" shoes hadn't yet been invented.

Over the ensuing years, the running boom began, and thousands of recreational athletes starting running marathons. It was during those early years that I experienced the true joy of running. The fun, camaraderie, and shared experience of training with other runners and crossing the finish line with them as they attained their goals was much more enjoyable than achieving any personal running goals of mine.

Saturday I watched my friends run Grandma's Marathon. I was signed up to run this year. It would have been my 90th marathon, and 25th Grandma's. Lisa Buhr, a running friend from Menomonie, told me last fall that she needed to sign up for Grandma's this year as motivation to train and get into shape. I had just finished chemotherapy and radiation for my tongue cancer and needed a goal to work toward. We signed up together and vowed to train and run this year's race together.

Three years ago, Lisa ran her very first marathon at Grandma's, and I ran it with her. Her unabashed joy at having completed her first marathon was inspiring and a greater reward than anything I could have done that day. Saturday she crossed the finish line in 3 hours 50 minutes, a personal record for her. When we met up after the race she cried, and no words were needed. Her tears were a demonstration of sadness and kindness, knowing how much I would have enjoyed running the race with her.

It has been two months since I last ran. I have lost twenty- five pounds and muscle strength and endurance. I haven't lost my joy of the camaraderie that is such a large part of distance running. The group of runners that faithfully meets on Saturday mornings to run and then go out for coffee is still a highlight of my week, even if I can only walk now.

I will continue to join my running friends for walks and watch their races. My friends gave me a Grandma's marathon jacket along with personal letters of thanks for all of the years of encouragement and running together. It was better than any "finisher" t-shirt or medallion.

When we get to the point where enjoying the success of others is more important than our own success, we find our greatest joy.

Meanwhile, that small ninth grade boy who ended up running cross country has learned that God still works in "strange and mysterious" ways. What can start out as disappointment can turn into a great blessing. God's plan is not always obvious to us at the time. Even with cancer, there is still hope for the future.

"FOR I KNOW THE PLANS I HAVE FOR YOU," SAYS THE LORD. "THEY ARE PLANS FOR GOOD AND NOT FOR DISASTER, TO GIVE YOU A FUTURE AND A HOPE." Jeremiah 29:11.

***

What do you think when people with very good health habits develop serious illness or an early death?

Do you blame those with poor health habits for their chronic illnesses?

Which groups do you belong to that share a common pastime or interest? Are these group members some of your closest friends?

Looking at your best friends, what has created these strong friendships?

What is the benefit, if any, of contributing to the success of others?

5. Marathon and beyond, or, "If it's worth doing, it's worth doing to excess."

July 1, 2014

As a family physician, some would believe that I should preach moderation in all things. Moderation is usually good. Many addictions have their initial roots in lack of moderation.

Yet, it can be argued that anything worth doing and worth doing well is worth doing to excess. At least, that's what you try to tell yourself when you decide that instead of just running more marathons, you are going to leap into the small but growing world of ultra-marathons (any race longer than 26.2 miles). In the Bible, St. Paul did say to "pray constantly" (I Thess. 5:17), so even God wasn't entirely into the moderation thing that we family docs are supposed to preach.

I ran several 50-mile races on the Gunflint Trail in northern Minnesota in the early 1980's with Kevin Peterson, a good friend from college. My interest in running ultra-marathons was re-kindled in 1999 when I entered the 100 km (62 miles) Del Passatore race in northern Italy. It was an enchanting event as I ran through Italian mountain villages on a night illuminated by a full moon. Wine was served as a drink option at the last two aid stations. When I finished, I was awarded three bottles of local Italian vino.

I started to wonder if my next challenge could be a 100-mile race. I entered the Rocky Raccoon 100 miler in Huntsville, TX, in 2000. Several miles into the race, I struck up a conversation with a veteran Canadian ultra-runner. I asked him, "What can I expect in my first 100-mile race?" He didn't mince any words, saying, "Something is going to go wrong, and then you will find out what you are made of." He presented a litany of possible issues that might occur, and it was quite prophetic. At mile 17, my foot twisted on the side of a root, and caused an ankle sprain. I ended up wrapping it with duct tape, as a medical worker looked on remarking, "In Texas we say, if the bone ain't showin', you keep on goin'." I finished, but it was the most difficult physical challenge that I had ever undertaken.

I eventually ran 35 ultra-marathons, including fourteen 100-mile races. The 100-milers take all day and all night with food and drink supplied at aid stations every 5-6 miles. Head lamps are needed to light the trail at night. The courses are interesting and beautiful, run on trails through the woods, over mountains and snow, by lakes and through streams. The challenge of completing 100 miles is so difficult that I once again felt the same butterflies in my stomach that I used to feel at the start of a marathon twenty years earlier. The excitement and thrill of running had returned.

My three most memorable 100-mile races were run alongside three of my closest friends. Greg Kleindl and I finished in Umstead State Park (Raleigh, NC) running through a cold, wind-driven rainy night. We put on every bit of clothing that we had to survive the blustery night, when most runners had to stop because of hypothermia. This race proved one adage of Wisconsin running: There is no such thing as bad weather, just bad clothing.

Rolf Morck and I finished the Burning River 100-miler (Cuyahoga Falls, OH) together after Rolf ran strong through the toughest section of race course that I had ever seen. At 80 miles, we entered a loop where rain had turned the trail to shoe-sucking mud. Rolf, who had grown up running and hiking the rocky Superior Hiking Trail on the north shore of Lake Superior, was like a mountain goat, bounding side to side to avoid the thick mud trail. I could barely keep up.

Finally, I had the privilege of running with Terry Sullivan to the finish line at the Vermont 100-miler. It was a 92-

degree day, and the course was hilly. When we reached 98 miles, he had two hours to finish under the 30 hour cut-off time. He was totally spent. We walked the last two miles in one hour 15 minutes to finish the race. I have never seen anyone more tired in my life. He said if the course had been one step longer, he wouldn't have finished it.

Why do I run 100- mile races? Because I can. Because completing a 100- mile race is a celebration of God's gift of good health, a motivator to train and stay healthy. Because overcoming adversity alongside another runner creates a special bond of friendship.

It is healthy for all of us to create goals and then to find the motivation and perseverance to attain them. It builds resilience. If I can train my body and mind to run 100 miles, I can train my mind to overcome many of life's obstacles. I feel youthful and thankful when I cross the finish line of a 100- mile race, knowing that it is an incredibly tough challenge, even for an experienced distance runner.

I remember taking chemotherapy last fall. The fatigue, nausea and the need to eat to keep going reminded me of the feeling I get during the last 30 miles of a 100- mile race. I could make it to the finish line in those races, and I knew I could make it to the end of chemotherapy and radiation.

I am taking chemotherapy again, and maybe those challenging ultras have really been training for the tougher ultra that includes surgery, chemo, head and neck radiation and cancer itself.

In the Bible, St. Paul reminds us that *"WE REJOICE IN OUR SUFFERINGS, KNOWING THAT SUFFERING PRODUCES ENDURANCE, AND ENDURANCE PRODUCES CHARACTER, AND CHARACTER PRODUCES HOPE, AND HOPE DOES NOT DISAPPOINT US, BECAUSE GOD'S LOVE HAS BEEN POURED INTO OUR HEARTS THROUGH THE HOLY SPIRIT WHICH HAS BEEN GIVEN TO US."* Romans 5:3-5

Peace be with you.

***

What are the things in your life that are worth doing to excess?

What are your goals in life?

What motivates you?

What are some of the toughest challenges that you have faced in life? How did you overcome those challenges?

How has one challenge prepared you for another?

6. What if....?"

July 10, 2014

Our family spent the 4th of July weekend at our cabin in Minnesota. It has been the family summer meeting place for decades with my parents, siblings, and our children gathering for water sports, conversation and relaxation.

While sitting on the deck, my dad made the comment, "What if we hadn't built this cabin forty-eight years ago?" Forty nine years ago, on May 6th, 1965, three tornadoes swept through Fridley, Minnesota destroying much of our hometown. It was a tragic event, as many families lost their homes and suffered injuries. My dad received an interesting invitation. The owner of two new apartment complexes, which were partially destroyed, offered to let my dad salvage any building materials he wanted.

That was a moment of opportunity for a Lutheran pastor who had wanted to someday build a cabin but didn't have the means to do it. Now he was able to purchase land on a lake and construct a cabin out of salvaged lumber, sheathing, windows and many other items that he pulled out of that tornado wreckage.

Had that tornado not occurred, our family probably would not have spent as much time together over the years. My dad would not have learned the building trades which eventually were handed down to his children and grandchildren.

When our boys were growing up, they both wanted to play high school football. Menomonie had a strong football program. Nathan was able to play and has benefited by learning the discipline of weight lifting and teamwork that were at the core of that program. He has gone on to complete a degree in mechanical engineering and works in Houston, TX.

as a far different story. He suffered a severe fracture-dislocation during his sophomore football season. The healing was slow. He struggled as he tried to play basketball and run track. His limited ability to play sports affected his mood and his schoolwork.

Almost a year after the injury, his ankle still hurting, he quit football. He came home from his final practice and said "I can't be an athlete. I guess I will just have to be a student." He was sad and frustrated at the prospect of not being able to play sports in high school.

From that day forward, he reinvented himself. He became a good student with an interest in learning that has persisted through college and into grad school. He developed new friendships. His compassion toward others who weren't popular or who needed help became more evident. He learned to play guitar and worked as a counselor at Luther Park Bible Camp. He liked being around the older counselors and graduated from high school a half year early to start college. In college, he eventually had enough healing of his ankle to play Ultimate Frisbee, intramural basketball and even run a few marathons with me.

What if Eric hadn't fractured his ankle? He would have missed out on many great experiences. His transformation to someone interested in life-long learning and his compassion toward others may have been far less robust.

Bad things happen to good people. We must always look for good in the bad, for opportunity in tragedy, and for new beginnings as other situations come to an end.

Although a destructive tornado and painful ankle fracture altered the course of our lives, we can now look back with thanksgiving that these events opened up the opportunity for some very good changes. We often go through life not realizing the far-reaching consequences of our decisions and how they will affect our future.

It is my hope and prayer that something good can come from my illness, even one as devastating as cancer. My focus for the remainder of my life is not how long I will live or how much I can do. As Amy and I prepare for my death, the process of dying has instead created a new opportunity to share God's spirit and to be recipients of God's grace through the kindness of others.

Peace be with you.

***

As you reflect on tragic or difficult events in your life, what good things were made possible through your struggle?

If you are led through a long dying process with a disease like cancer, what good would you want to see come out of your struggle at the end of life?

How does it make you feel if someone says "If God shuts a door, He opens a window" in the midst of a crisis or difficult situation?

7. Living with cancer, or dying from cancer?

July 19, 2014

My current chemotherapy started just two days after a clinic visit with my oncologist Dr. Sandeep Basu, and my palliative care specialist and family physician colleague, Dr. Jim Deming. At the time of that visit, I had been experiencing increasing pain in my neck and jaw. Narcotic pain relievers were only partially effective. With a prognosis of approximately 6-9 months left in life, it was hard to fathom that I could live with pain for that long. I was questioning the wisdom of chemotherapy which might prolong my painful life.

My goals were made clear. I wanted less pain. How long I continued to live wasn't the priority. The quality of life remaining was far more important than the number of months left in life.

Fortunately, the wisdom of both physicians prevailed at that visit. They encouraged me to go ahead with chemotherapy, noting that halting the aggressively growing cancer would likely lessen the pain. I am happy to report that two months later the pain has decreased. I experience side effects from the chemo, most notably mouth soreness which keeps me on a pureed and liquid diet. The trade-off, however, has been a good one with chemo side-effects less severe than the cancer pain itself.

What does less pain really mean for Amy and me? It means we can enjoy time with friends and family and do some limited travel. I feel like being more active and engaged. Mood is better and a desire to live longer has returned. I am thankful that God has allowed a period of time when pain isn't the consuming issue of each day.

Sometimes we ask the question, "Is your cup half empty or half full?" I am a cup half- full person who is generally optimistic about life and life changes. I will continue to say that I am living with cancer instead of dying from cancer.

I often read in obituaries that a person "lost his battle with cancer." Our deaths are inevitable as part of the circle of life. When my chemotherapy quits working, I will not be focused on a losing battle with cancer. Instead I will invite hospice into our home and live out the final stage of life with family and friends close by.

I am thankful and at peace with my life. Amy and I are preparing for a large number of guests who are coming to my retirement party at our house. I am thankful for the good friends who helped clean our house and garage and set up for the event. Of course there are higher priorities in life than a spotlessly clean and de-cluttered house. We will focus on enjoying the company of colleagues that I have worked with over the years at Mayo Clinic Health System-Red Cedar. It is a day to look forward to when you are living with cancer.

Peace be with you.

***

Are you a "cup half-empty" or "cup half-full" person?

We often hear the words battle and fight when talking about a person's journey with cancer. In what ways could using terms like this make it difficult to be accepting of dying with a protracted illness like cancer?

8. M&Ms in a bottle

July 27, 2014

I remember one of Amy's many methods of parenting. As our sons approached their teenage years, she told them about one of the developmental tests for child brain development. M&Ms were placed in a bottle. Very young toddlers will try to stick their fingers into the bottle to remove the M&Ms. They are unsuccessful. An older child will simply turn the bottle upside down and dump out the candy. She explained to our boys that the brain hadn't developed far enough for the young toddler to understand the easy way to remove the M&Ms from the bottle.

In our household, we insisted that our boys always wear bike helmets, buckle up in the car, look both ways crossing the street, etc. Teenage boys don't always have safety and prevention of bodily harm as their first priority. When they didn't, Amy would gently remind them of their current stage of brain development saying, "You're trying to grab M&Ms from the bottom of a bottle."

Although we have a tendency to believe that our brain development occurs during childhood, the brain continues to develop throughout adulthood. The ability to accept and even embrace death at the end of life is a stage of development seen in many elderly people, particularly those whose quality of life has deteriorated.

As a family physician, I had many opportunities to discuss the process of death with patients and their families. Many patients, particularly those with a Christian faith and belief in heaven were quite accepting of the end of their journey on earth. Many had experienced a decline in health because of illness and/or age. They hadn't given up on life but had reached the point where their deterioration of their health, belief in God and the inevitability of death created a trifecta that embraced death.

In this scenario, it was not uncommon for family members to want us to do more to keep their loved one alive and to use whatever medical means were available to prolong life. It was difficult to accept that their loved one was truly ready to depart from this world and the companionship of their family.

Accepting death, however, is more than simply a developmental process of the brain. To truly befriend death, we must lay claim to be children of God and to see our death as a path to new life.

Beyond that, we should cherish the thought that our lives live on in those whom we have touched in meaningful ways. Our acts of kindness, generosity, faith and love towards others don't go unnoticed. Instead, they are the greatest inheritance that our friends and family can receive.

***

Whose lives do you think you have touched in a meaningful way?

In Romans 8:18 Paul says, "I consider that the sufferings of this present time are not worth comparing with the glory that is to be revealed to us." Has your faith in heaven matured to the point of accepting the inevitability of death followed by a better life in heaven?

9. An African curse

August 2, 2014

Perhaps the most amazing event that occurred when Amy and I were in Cameroon began with a C-section delivery of a healthy baby boy. The Cameroonian mother had been in labor for days in a nearby village. Much to my surprise, when I delivered the baby's head up through the lower abdominal incision, it was covered with a layer of gray mud. Unbeknownst to me, a witch doctor had been packing mud into the patient's birth canal, hoping it would "draw" the baby out of the womb.

I was a stickler when it came to operating room cleanliness. Every day the two African surgical assistants and I cleaned and scrubbed the operating room from top to bottom. But when mud and grit appeared on the baby's head and now contaminated the mother's entire abdomen, even the surgical assistant knew we were in trouble. We did everything possible to clean and rinse the abdomen and pelvis. Fortunately, with the use of IV antibiotics and another operation to drain an abscess, as well as many prayers for healing, the mother survived.

Because she had been sick with the post-operative infection and was on IV antibiotics, she didn't breastfeed her baby. That was unusual in Cameroon, but didn't present a problem since infant formula was readily available through our pharmacy.

The mother and infant were discharged from the hospital, both doing well, only to return a couple of days later. The infant was lethargic and dehydrated and had lost a significant amount of weight. The mother assured me that they had picked up the formula, bottles, nipples—everything needed to formula feed an infant.

The baby was re-hydrated at the hospital and gained weight rapidly. I couldn't identify any physical problem with the infant and he was once again discharged home. Feeding instructions were reviewed with the mother who had fed the infant while in the hospital.

We saw the infant boy back just one day later. He had lost weight again, and was very fussy and hungry. I now asked the obvious question, "Are you feeding him at home?" The mother's answer was, "No." "Why not?" I asked.

The mother's answer stunned me. She reported that when she was pregnant, her husband, while riding on his moped, accidentally hit and killed a neighbor's dog. The neighbor was furious and had placed a "curse" on the unborn child, saying that he would die. Consequently, there was no reason to feed her baby since he was going to die anyway.

At this point, I needed help. I needed someone who understood the power and meaning of a Cameroonian curse. It was time for one of our missionaries to step in.

Our missionary friend told the mother that she had a choice. God is much more powerful than any curse or ill-will that a neighbor might place on her. She should feed her baby and allow God the opportunity to grow and strengthen the child. She truly had a choice and was not bound by her neighbor's curse.

With the mother now feeding formula to her infant, he did flourish. When Amy and I left Cameroon, he was developing normally, and the mother was very happy.

We also have a choice: How strongly do we believe in God and God's power over evil? Are we more focused on hopelessness and negative, destructive thinking? Although none of us would refuse to feed a child because of a "curse," do we allow fear to rule our hearts and minds? In fact, it is probably much easier in U. S. society than African society to choose priorities other than our faith in God. We can easily allow our busy lives to crowd out God and to become distracted. Although that may not sound as awful as allowing a newborn to die, our separation from God can become just as profound.

We have a choice. Let's use it to center our lives and life's decisions on God and God's goodness. Let us keep our hearts and minds firmly focused on the power and promises of God. We have no better thoughts than those that are centered on God.

***

How has the busy-ness of American life distracted you and separated you from God?

What are your biggest priorities in life?

What are negative of destructive thoughts that prevent you from being the hope-filled person you desire to be?

10. Plans for the future

August 8, 2014

Years ago, someone asked me what disease would be the worst cause of death. I shudder today when I remember that my answer was "a head and neck cancer." I was the hospice medical director during my early years in Menomonie. I vividly recall a couple patients who died with head and neck cancers. They suffered with pain that wasn't easy to control, and eventually the cancers invaded vital structures involved with eating, talking, swallowing and breathing.

Although it is not pleasant to imagine that the end of my life will be similar to theirs, there are some advantages to having cancer.

I had assumed that someday I would likely suffer a heart attack. My family history includes a brother who had a heart attack at age 45, and my mother had one at age 62. Almost ten years ago, a chest CT scan showed that I had an increased amount of calcification in a major coronary artery. It appeared that I had inherited my family's predilection for heart disease.

Despite knowing that I was at risk for a sudden death from a heart attack, Amy and I did little to prepare for that possibility. When it comes to planning for death, it is easy to procrastinate. The diagnosis of cancer, however, has allowed time for us to plan for the end of life.

I am impressed by my parents' plans for death. They have always been people who didn't want to burden their children and are who aware that the execution of an estate plan sometimes tears families apart. Instead my parents have downsized to a small condominium with fewer furnishings. They have de-cluttered their home, have funeral services planned, obituaries written, grave sites and memorial stone purchased, and a file with all will, trust, advanced directives and other financial or key documents that are needed.

Many grieving families are overwhelmed by the many tasks and decisions that accompany a death. Because of my parents' planning, our family will not be counted among the overwhelmed.

Amy and I now find ourselves doing many of the things that my parents have already done to prepare for death. We also understand that many of our household tasks are done by only one of us and not by both of us. If Amy were to die suddenly, we realize that I am not the cook, the gardener or the social activities director of our household. As we plan for my death, we realize that I have been the one to invest savings, keep files, file taxes and use tools to build or fix things. Amy is now working to master those skills.

While all of these preparations will help the transition to widowhood, a more important preparation is taking place. We are reconnecting with old friends, and having meaningful conversations with family and friends. We have a sense of gratitude for the lives we have been given.

Our sons and my parents live far away, but we have cherished the opportunity to see them more often. Amy and I have enjoyed more time together, further strengthening our bond of marriage. We have appreciated this extra time together and have spent time with family and friends. We feel blessed to be able to do the things that are important to us. We are grateful for not having to deal with the issues surrounding a sudden, unexpected death.

We shouldn't need a cancer diagnosis to do all of these things but a cancer diagnosis has been the impetus to plan ahead. As Amy and I live with cancer, we will continue to count our blessings and to appreciate the opportunity it has brought to plan for the future.

Peace be with you.

***

What preparations have you made for the end of your life?

If you or your partner were to die suddenly, would it be overwhelming because of a lack of preparation?

Would the amount your possessions you leave behind be overwhelming for your family to manage?

If you could choose, would you prefer to die quickly, as in a sudden accident, or gradually, as in the case of cancer? What are the advantages/disadvantages of each?

11. "We're with Dave"

August 16, 2014

In psychology, it is said that we develop our self-image by what we perceive that others think about us. The perception may not be accurate, but our self-image is based on our perception. If I think that those around me like me and care for me, I develop a strong and confident self-image. If I believe that those around me don't like me, I develop low self-esteem. An understanding of how self-image is developed is especially important for parents as they must show love but still discipline their children without breaking their will and lowering their self-esteem.

Last weekend Amy and I spent several days with a group of friends. One of those days included a trip to Wisconsin Dells. Our friends Dan and Kerri Wood brought along a pile of tee-shirts that they had made for the occasion. The front of the tee-shirt said, "We're with Dave." The back showed a group of runners with a phrase in Norwegian: "Kjør ræva av i livet!" Translated it reads "Run your ass off in life."

Apparently if the group had to pick a credo for my life, this is it. I will admit that I have packed a lot into my fifty-seven years and it includes running both literally and figuratively. Amy and I have used many similar sayings over the years: "If you can't run with the big dogs, stay on the porch." "If you are not living on the edge, you are taking up too much space." "Go big or stay home." "Go fast, take chances." Our sons wanted to interpret the last one as "Drive fast, take chances," so it was never used again. We aren't guaranteed good health or a long life, so all of these sayings are reminders that we need to be active and adventurous in life.

I am not at a point in life where my self-image is forming, but there is never a time in life when self-image isn't influenced by the words and actions of others. I marvel at the love and attention that people have given to our family, knowing that it is a difficult time of life. Visits, conversations, cards, flowers, prayer shawls, food, CaringBridge posts and the offer to help in any way possible are not just appreciated, but have helped us to feel good, even on days when cancer or chemotherapy doesn't leave me feeling good physically.

I am impressed that we live in a community where so many people are willing to help or aid others. There is a compounding effect to being on the receiving end of that generosity. Amy and I feel like we also want to be more generous towards others, knowing how good it has felt to be recipients of friends' love and care.

If "Run your ass off in life" is a motto for my life, then it is something that I want to do with and for the benefit of others. Actions speak louder than words. That friends took the time to make a tee-shirt and spend vacation time with us was more important than the words on the shirt. We are thankful for all the kindness that has been brought into our lives.

Peace be with you.

***

How would you describe your self-image?

How do you perceive you are viewed by others?

How do your words/actions directed toward others affect their self-image?

12. Luther Park Bible Camp—Nurturing faith through holy play

August 21, 2014

Two weeks ago, we attended the annual Luther Park Bible Camp quilt and craft auction in Chetek, Wisconsin. Our family has a long tradition with Luther Park Bible Camp. Amy and I met there when we worked as camp counselors.

We first met at a camp counselor retreat in the spring of 1978. It was an opportunity for summer counselors to meet each other. Lisa Novotny, a friend of mine at Augsburg College, already knew Amy and said, "You are going to like Amy Kaste." That was an understatement.

Amy remembers that I made a dramatic first impression that weekend. We were all playing some crazy game when it was dark outside, and I ran full speed into a barbed wire fence. Amy took me to the emergency room to get fixed up with bandages and a tetanus booster.

In 1978 we were two out of four counselors who worked at a primitive teepee village called Luther Woods near Birchwood, Wisconsin. In 1979 we were the two trip counselors who took senior high youth on more adventurous trips that included canoeing, backpacking and camping. We both loved being camp counselors and Amy would say with a sense of awe, "We get paid for doing this?"

In 1992 Luther Park tore down its old cabins and replaced them with new ones. The three ELCA Lutheran churches in Menomonie offered to build one of the cabins. It took six months to build, and we had sixty-five different volunteers who helped build it. It was a great opportunity for mixed generations to work together and to develop a connection with the camp.

Amy and I made twenty weekend trips up to Luther Park with our two young sons to help build the cabin. The kids were usually full of dirt, mud or snow by the end of the work day. One time our van got a flat tire as it got stuck in a thick mud puddle at the camp. It only got worse when our son Nathan hit the door lock, closed the van door, and locked all of us outside of the van with the engine and heater running. A locksmith was required to remedy that problem but it didn't stop us from getting a full day of construction done with our group of volunteers.

As our boys were growing up, we attended a week of family camp for fifteen straight summers. Many of the same families attended each year, which created a sense of community that endeared us to this annual vacation. We could have afforded more exotic or extravagant vacations but found that there was no better family vacation than a week at Bible camp. Eric even followed in our footsteps and eventually became a Luther Park camp counselor.

Amy spends a couple weekends at camp each year with a group of women who work on quilts and other sewing projects. No "boys" are allowed. I hear that a lot of coffee and chocolate are consumed, and that sleep is an overrated experience. At their last quilt retreat, she met Keith Newman, the newly hired camp director. When the sewer lines froze, Keith and the maintenance director Dave Dobbs, spent much of the day digging to thaw the frozen pipes. The camp is in good hands and is building on great tradition and leadership of years past. We are very happy to see the ministry at Luther Park grow and flourish.

Many kids who attend Luther Park Bible Camp go as part of their confirmation class. Some go willingly, some reluctantly. At the end of their week at camp almost all of them are sad to leave. There is something very powerful about a youth ministry where the counselors are young (college-aged), fun and energetic. They play music on guitar and keyboard, swim, play games, have campfires, lead Bible studies and serve as role models for kids that are at an impressionable age.

Amy and I feel nostalgic when we talk about Luther Park Bible Camp. It is a place that carries fond memories for our family. It is a place where we gladly volunteer our time, talents, and treasures to help further a ministry that is particularly meaningful to middle school teenagers, but also to people of all ages. It has given our family an opportunity to contribute to a ministry that is greater than ourselves. We all should be fortunate enough to have a place like Luther Park in our lives for retreat and renewal.

Amy and I are not the only couple that met at Luther Park. There are literally dozens of couples who met there and are now married. So if you have a child who decides to be a camp counselor, take a good look at the staff. You might be looking at a future in-law.

www.lutherpark.org

***

What is your favorite vacation?

What does that vacation give you that makes it your favorite?

Did you attend any camps as a child?

What are your remembrances of that experience?

Do you or your family contribute to a ministry?

What makes that ministry worthy of your support?

13. Fear of the unknown

August 29, 2014

Amy and I have twice ventured into underdeveloped countries to do medical missionary work. The first time was to Haiti at the end of medical school. We were accompanied by our good friends, Mark and Bev Deyo-Svendsen. A combination of youthfulness, naiveté, prayer and having our friends at our side made us feel secure. Despite the third world experiences of overcrowded buses, maniac drivers and a motor vehicle accident that could have ended badly for all of us, we were never dissuaded from doing this again.

Traveling into Cameroon, Africa, didn't feel as safe. When we landed in the large port city of Douala, Cameroon, it was clear that our white-skinned American bodies smelled of wealth. Africans rushed to be the first at the airport to grab our luggage, get us a taxi and earn a tip. We didn't speak their language, and their aggressiveness was unnerving. Had we come through Douala alone, it would have been a scary experience. Instead the American Lutheran Church was wise in sending us with a veteran missionary couple to accompany us through the country. They taught us about bribing police to get us through checkpoints and began our enculturation into a country very different from the USA. Having a seasoned guide lead us through the unknown ventures of African travel was a great comfort.

As a family physician, the fear of the unknown was a real worry for patients. They would come in with symptoms that required further testing. Waiting for test results was difficult particularly when it involved the possibility of serious illness. There were hundreds of times over the years when I would contact patients right away after critical tests, knowing that waiting for the test result produced anxiety.

What I found interesting was that sometimes, even if the news was bad, it was more comforting to *know* the test result and what it meant. The fear of not knowing was actually greater than knowing that we had now diagnosed a chronic disease which may plague the patient for the remainder of his life. If the news was very bad, such as cancer, it would typically be delivered face-to-face with a spouse or family member present to provide comfort, to ask questions, and to have a second set of ears. The message was delivered with a plan for treatment, referral to a different specialist, and a promise that we would do everything possible to help. Even very bad news sometimes provided relief from anxiety knowing that there was a plan laid out for the future.

I believe that fear of death is often fear of the unknown. We do not want to leave what is familiar and emotionally comfortable. We grieve the loss of relationships to family and friends. Although a large majority of Americans believe in heaven or an afterlife, we aren't sure how that will look or feel. In some ways, it's like that trip to Africa where you really aren't sure what to expect.

The Bible describes heaven as a restoration of all things, involving the removal of every sinful impurity and the retaining of all that is holy and good. There should be no more death, sorrow, crying or pain. Because the Bible describes something that we don't experience in this world, we can't fully comprehend it. Some people may even think that it will be a little boring flying around with winged angels playing a harp (not a Biblical concept).

Jesus spoke of heaven as being a home of many rooms that He has prepared for us. Biblical saints looked forward to heaven. There is nothing written in the Bible that suggests that we shouldn't look forward to heaven as well.

We have more than the Bible as a witness to what lies beyond death. There are many accounts of patients who describe positive near-death experiences. These accounts include experiencing passage through a tunnel toward light, meeting relatives who died before them, or seeing one's life flash before one's eyes. Some report observing the medical team performing resuscitation efforts as if they were floating above and out of their bodies. They experience a sense of inner peace, well-being and painlessness that is very real to them before regaining consciousness. At recovery back to life, they usually have lost any fear of death. For some individuals, these accounts are relegated to be the musings of people whose oxygen-deprived brains created a comforting state of delirium. For many Christians, including myself, these experiences are believed to be a small appetizer or taste of heaven given before the full meal.

Several people recently have been compelled to tell me their stories of near-death experience with the goal of providing some comfort for me. I believe their stories, and appreciate their openness and willingness to share their experience.

Just like the veteran missionary couple that guided Amy and me through the unknown on our trip to Cameroon, we have the Bible and the experience of others who have survived near-death to guide us through death into a new life. And the best companion we have to walk with us to death is Jesus. We should not be afraid.

"LET NOT YOUR HEARTS BE TROUBLED; BELIEVE IN GOD, BELIEVE ALSO IN ME. IN MY FATHER'S HOUSE ARE MANY ROOMS; IF IT WERE NOT SO, WOULD I HAVE TOLD YOU THAT I GO TO PREPARE A PLACE FOR YOU? AND WHEN I GO AND PREPARE A PLACE FOR YOU, I WILL COME AGAIN AND WILL TAKE YOU TO MYSELF, THAT WHERE I AM YOU MAY BE ALSO."

JOHN 14: 1-3

***

What is it about death that makes some of us fearful?

Have you or someone you know ever told you about a near-death experience?

What do you think is the meaning behind, or explanation of, these experiences?

14. American Cancer Society Relay for Life in Menomonie

September 7, 2014

I was asked to give an introductory talk at the American Cancer Society Relay for Life event in Menomonie last Friday night. It was an opportunity to talk about the importance of cancer research and our need to press on in developing safe and effective cancer treatments.

Virtually everyone lives a life touched by cancer. That includes one of three women, and one out of two men developing some form of cancer during their lifetime in the United States. Nearly one out of four Americans will die from cancer.

Our family experienced cancer on both ends of the spectrum. My wife Amy developed a thyroid cancer twenty-five years ago that was easily surgically removed, and the chance of her cancer returning was <1%. One year ago, I developed tongue cancer, and was treated with surgery, chemotherapy, and radiation. I am still on chemotherapy but the cancer has spread now beyond the ability to cure it.

Many cancer treatments are brutal. Unfortunately, we are still looking forward to the day when cancer treatments will target only cancer cells, and will not affect healthy tissues.

Although we have come a long way in cancer treatment, we still have a long way to go. One hundred years ago, if you went to see a surgeon to have a tumor removed, the surgery was done with a scalpel blade that the surgeon carried around in his back pocket all day. If you got an infection, there was no antibiotic to cure it. Many healthcare workers who administered radiation died from exposure because it was so difficult to direct the radiation to the correct areas. Chemotherapy was non-existent 100 years ago. We are fortunate to be living with much improved cancer treatments today, but we still have the same difficulties in targeting just cancer cells. Solving this problem is a major area of current research.

The cancer genome project began in 2003, and it aims to identify and track the genes that produce cancer. The next step will be to use that information to truly target cancer cells and not the healthy cells that are currently being damaged by chemotherapy and radiation. We also will be able to better identify which therapy works best on specific genetic mutations. New therapies that target cancer genes or boost the cancer patient's immune system to help destroy cancer cells are already being developed.

We scoff at the medical practices 100 years ago, such as the use of leeches, blood-letting, purges, arsenic and mercury to treat illness. Yet future generations will someday look back at our current cancer treatments, and view them as being barbaric.

That is why the American Cancer Society (ACS) sponsors fund-raising events all around the country. Although the ACS does much more than raise money for research, cancer research has become one of the most exciting areas of medical research today. The gains that we expect in the future are going to be huge.

I also wanted to say on behalf of our family how appreciative we have been to live in a community like Menomonie. The cards, letters, visits, prayers, prayer shawls, and flowers have been wonderful. We really feel grateful and loved by such a caring community.

We are also grateful to have the Mayo Clinic Health System nearby. I have worked as a physician in that system for the last fifteen years, and I have seen the collaboration in cancer care, particularly among the specialists. I can tell you that personally, it was great to be able to go to Rochester. We have the most famous and arguably the most advanced clinic in the world. If you go down there, you know that people come from all over the world to be treated at a place that is less than a two hour drive from here. I had all of my radiation treatment through Mayo in

Eau Claire, and am delighted to have all of my chemotherapy done here in Menomonie. We have a great nursing staff, and there is no other place that I would rather be for chemotherapy than in our hometown of Menomonie.

With that, I would like to welcome all of you on behalf of the Mayo Clinic Health System. As someone living with cancer, I want to thank all of you for being here, and supporting a worthy cause.

***

How has your life been touched by cancer?

Why do you think so many people develop cancer?

Why is it so difficult to cure cancer?

Should the government direct more funds for cancer research?

15. The Making of a Doctor

September 13, 2014

PBS and NOVA produced a television documentary in 2000 titled, "MD: The Making of a Doctor." It followed seven Harvard medical students from their excitement of starting medical school through the competitive academic rigor of medical training. A sequel continued to follow them through the harsh realities of residency into medical practice where exhausting training schedules had left too little time for family. I recall that six out of the seven students ended up divorced. I am thankful that my wife Amy tolerated those years of training when learning the practice of medicine seemed all consuming.

Over the years, I allowed high school and college students who were interested in becoming a physician spend a day with me in clinic or in the emergency room. I often loaned them my video of "MD: The Making of a Doctor." I wanted them to have a full picture of life while in training to become a physician. Although the documentary showed the intensity of training, it also showed that training to be a physician could be a rewarding experience.

I started at Augsburg College as a math major. I realized early on that I liked math because I was good at it and not because I saw myself in a math career. By my sophomore year, I had decided to become a chemistry professor, but I wasn't entirely sold on this major either. My organic chemistry professor encouraged me to stay in chemistry and lamented that his best students often went to medical school. He told me that if I became a physician, I would affect the lives of hundreds of people. If I became a chemist, I could affect the lives of millions of people.

In college, I never had the experience of doing meaningful research as part of a research team. Our son Eric is now in chemistry grad school at the University of Iowa, and his research is both interesting and relevant. I suspect that I would be a chemist today if I had participated in practical and meaningful research during college. Instead, I made the decision in my junior year to attend medical school. I took the MCAT (Medical College Admission Test) and applied to the University of Minnesota-Duluth School of Medicine under an early decision program. Less than five months after deciding to become a physician, I was admitted to medical school.

I must admit that I knew little about the long workdays and nights of a medical resident when I decided to become a physician. I spent some time in my junior year at college tagging along with a family physician. I was sure that I wanted to do what he did, regardless of the process to get there. Medical school just reinforced my desire to be a family physician as I worked alongside family physicians that seemed in tune with their patients' needs, not just as managers of disease.

The training hours to become a physician are long. The specialty of family medicine requires four years of medical school and a three-year residency program. Those years made college look like an extended vacation.

In residency, it was very common to take overnight call, working the day before and after, a shift that lasted up to 36 hours. Residency regulations enacted a decade ago restrict medical residents from working more than 30 continuous hours without a 10-hour break and forbid working more than an 80-hour workweek averaged over four weeks. Those are still long workweeks but are a much needed improvement.

Sleep deprivation was so severe in residency that sometimes when I was awoken on overnight call, I wouldn't remember conversing or giving an order over the phone with hospital nursing staff. Scary, but fortunately I didn't make any bad decisions over the phone, even when I was too tired to remember a nighttime conversation the next morning. Sometimes it was hard to wake up during the night. When working at the Sioux Falls VA Hospital, I was often the only physician on-call at night. When a code blue (patient's heart or breathing stopped) occurred, a police siren and flashing lights were mounted over my bed to make sure that my heart was pounding as I shot out of bed and responded quickly to the emergency at hand.

There are many parents who would like to see their child become a physician. But unless that child has a strong internal drive to help others, to study hard, to work long hours, and to forego free time while in their 20s, it is best to steer clear of medical school.

Most family physicians enjoy their work, and I am one of them. The Wisconsin Academy of Family Physicians in a 2013 survey reported that 82% of its members would become family physicians if they had to do it all over again. Even though pay, prestige and work hours may not be as good as other specialties, there is no substitute for the trusting relationships with patients that are built over many shared experiences. For me to be at midlife and still to find joy, enthusiasm and fulfillment in my calling as a family physician was to live a privileged life.

I believe that most college students would benefit by having career counseling. It is no easier to choose a career today than when I was in college almost forty years ago. I now realize that a career in chemistry could have been rewarding and meaningful, but I have never regretted the decision to become a family physician.

***

What career or job gave you the most joy and fulfillment?

Would you choose a different career, if you had your life to do over?

Do students today receive enough information or career counseling to guide them to a wise career choice?

Why do so many people hope that their children will become a physician? What does that say about our society?

16. Fritz and Spidey

September 23, 2014

Last night I spent a couple of hours on the phone with Dave Bratt, my best friend while growing up. When we talk on the phone, I sometimes feel like a chatty teen-aged girl with conversations rarely lasting less than one hour.

Dave's high school nickname was "Fritz." This name was given to him by our seventh-grade German language teacher who gave everyone in her class a German name. My name was Wilhelm. Thank goodness it didn't stick! Instead, my nickname was "Spidey." In seventh-grade, "Eitrheim" morphed from "Speedy Eitrheim" into "Speedy Eity" and finally "Spidey." Some teachers even called me Spidey, but if I pick up the phone today and hear the name Spidey, I can be sure that Fritz is on the line.

Best friends talk about anything and everything. Conversation can take any direction. Unlike most other friendships, there aren't just one to two favorite topics or common interests to discuss.

Fritz and I walked together to junior and senior high school instead of taking the bus. If you ever want to develop a friendship, nothing beats walking together which seems to act like a relief valve that spews conversation.

Fritz and I once rode our bikes to a shopping mall. Ten-speed bicycles were being stolen at the time so we locked our two bikes tightly together with three chains and padlocks. When we came out of the mall, Fritz's shiny new ten-speed bike was gone, and even the chains and locks weren't spared. The only thing remaining was my cheap Schwinn three-speed bike, with upright handlebars and baskets on the side. Fritz's look of disbelief told it all as he said, "Spidey, your bike is still here!" How considerate of Fritz to have a nice bike that distracted thieves away from my scrap of metal.

Recently two events have brought us closer together. Fritz's 88-year-old father is in his final days in a hospice unit with cancer and kidney failure. I am living with cancer and experiencing a slow decline.

There are some similarities when Fritz and I talk about my cancer and his father's aging. In many ways I feel like my body has aged twenty to thirty years in this past year. Like an old man, I often wear extra layers of clothing to stay warm. I have wrinkles in my skin where fat and muscle have diminished. I sleep poorly, waking up multiple times each night and napping in the afternoon. I am weak. I chopped wood last week and had to rest after every 4-5 swings. I have developed "chemo brain": my mind isn't sharp, and I forget names and words more easily. Taking medication for pain is a daily experience. It is humbling to grow old.

I don't need or desire pity for the aging process that cancer and chemotherapy has caused. Having a body aged by cancer and its treatment doesn't diminish my desire to walk or to do physical work. I simply work more slowly and need more rest time.

The aging of my body from cancer has caused some good things to occur. The physical changes in my body have made me more empathetic toward others. In the news I can see someone suffering and feel emotional. There is a closeness that I feel when I see others who suffer or who are in pain. It is a human-ness that is good for the soul.

I am more reflective. With physical decline comes a level of spiritual renewal. I previously enjoyed a life of superb health. As my body fatigues, it is by faith that I realize that my decline in physical health is but a temporary state. While I can't halt the physical decline of my body, I needn't experience a spiritual decline as well.

Many people don't know what to say when someone has cancer or is very ill or dying. Just like a best friend, talking about anything and everything is just fine. Having cancer or ill health shouldn't create any new barriers to conversation. In fact, it could add some topics that many people avoid: death, grief, and spiritual beliefs. There is no need to cheer me up or strive to create new conversation based on my cancer.

Amy and I have spent more time recently with people from our past. There is nostalgia to spending this treasured time with old friends. Reminiscing about past events brings laughter and fuels my soul. When I hear "Hi, Spidey," I know that Fritz is at the other end of the phone, ready to talk about everything and anything. We all need that kind of a friend in our lives. When life isn't flowing as easily as it did in the past, I appreciate longtime friends more than ever.

Donald Herbert Bratt June 1, 1926 - September 25, 2014 Rest in peace.

***

Who is your best friend? What makes that relationship special?

Who is the friend you have known the longest?

Are their people you were friends with longer ago that you would like to see again?

What makes you feel empathy for others?

17. Skol Vikings

September 29, 2014

I am a Minnesota Vikings fan living in Packerland. Although Menomonie is only seventy miles from Minneapolis, this is Wisconsin, and Wisconsinites love their football team. I can't help myself. I grew up in suburban Minneapolis. I have fond childhood memories of our family watching Viking football games during the years when strong defenses led by the Purple People Eaters put the Vikings into four hapless Super Bowls.

My wife is a more avid football fan than I. She claims that it's because she is a loyal Packer backer and I am merely a sunny-day Viking fan. She scoffs at the claim that the Dallas Cowboys are "America's team." Our son Nathan is still a Cowboys fan, and alarmed his mother at an early age when he announced, "I like the stinking Dallas Cowboys." He had never heard of the Cowboys referred to in any other way and thought that "stinking" was part of the team name.

You have to be a loyal and hopelessly optimistic fan to still cheer for a team that hasn't won a championship in the 53-year history of the franchise. I have a friend who always wore an old Chicago Cubs baseball cap. He wasn't from Chicago but just liked underdogs. It put a smile on my face, knowing that the Cubs haven't won a championship in over 100 years. Flag poles were erected on the Wrigley Field roof to hold all of the Cub's future World Series pennants. Those flag poles have since rusted and been taken down. Viking fans, we are halfway through a Cubs century.

Amy and I used to bet on each Viking-Packer game. It began harmlessly enough, betting a movie or a dinner out. I took ballroom dancing classes and eventually bought Amy a horse, saddle and horse trailer off of Packer victories.

We had a swimming pool in our backyard with large oak trees littering leaves and acorns into the pool. I won the chance to cut the oaks down, but before I could fire up my chainsaw, Amy pleaded to go double or nothing on the next game. Her Packers won the oak trees back later in the season.

Apparently placing bets isn't my forte. I decided one year to ask for a trip to Northern Italy to vacation and to run an ultramarathon. The Vikings won, but I didn't sense any disappointment from Amy that she would now have to accompany me on a trip to Italy. The stakes were getting too big so we finally quit betting on the Viking-Packer games.

I sometimes go to Lambeau Field when Amy's extended family makes their annual pilgrimage to Green Bay. The last time I tried to enter Lambeau Field for a Packers game, I dressed in a Packer jersey. A security officer twice passed his metal detecting wand over me before he pulled me out of line for a complete pat-down. He finally let me through, and I quickly caught up to Said, a Lebanese man who had married our niece. "Said, this is profiling at Lambeau. They see a Viking fan disguised in Packer garb and frisk me while they let the Arab go right through." Security was never that stringent at the Metrodome. Even snow could collapse the roof and find its way into the stadium.

Being a Viking fan teaches us to humbly accept defeat. We are a true northern team. We start the season with the warmth, flowering and promise of summer in great expectation that this might be THE YEAR. We always end up with dashed hopes in the dead of a bitterly cold winter. We cheer for underdogs who in fairy tales end up as victors. Apparently pro football isn't a fairy tale.

Someday the Vikings will under-promise and over-deliver. Short of at least two miracles, I won't live to see that day. At least professional football is still only a game. After defeat, most fans aren't looking for the nearest bridge.

Even Packer fans sometimes sympathize with us Viking fans. Each year on a Friday before a Viking-Packer game, we were allowed to wear our team colors and jerseys to work. One of my Viking fan colleagues wore his Viking jersey accompanied by a bag over his head. Smart move to conceal his identity. Packer fans reacted with sympathy and laughter.

I will admit that the Green Bay Packers are my second favorite team. If the Vikings can't win it, I would like to see the Packers go all the way. I still live in Wisconsin, and I still love my wife.

***

Why do sports interest you (or not)?

How important is winning to you?

Does our society elevate sports and winning to a greater level of importance than it deserves?

Are there any ongoing sports rivalries in your family?

Why do we love an underdog?

18. A Biography of Cancer

October 6, 2014

I recently read the book, The Emperor of All Maladies: A Biography of Cancer, written by an oncologist Dr. Siddhartha Mukherjee.

Each form of cancer shares one common feature: the violent, uncontrollable growth of cells. The rogue cells spread to neighboring tissue through lymph channels and the bloodstream. Cancer is the human body battling itself.

Cancer treatment has a fascinating albeit cruel history. A century ago cancer was described as "a monster more insatiable than the guillotine." Treatments for cancer were often torturous. Up until 1948, there were two known treatments, surgery and radiation. The surgeries typically involved the removal of the cancer and all the normal surrounding tissue. Surgery was painful without modern-day anesthesia. Without sterile technique and in the era before antibiotics, post-operative infections were common and often led to premature deaths. Radiation was delivered in high doses to tumors and damaged everything in its wide destructive path.

Both surgery and radiation were ineffective once cancer had spread or metastasized. As one observer noted, "There were few successes in the treatment of disseminated cancer…. It was usually a matter of watching the tumor get bigger, and the patient, progressively smaller."

In 1948, Dr. Sidney Farber stumbled upon the first chemotherapy. Children suffering from leukemia were given the nutrient folic acid to stimulate the bone marrow production of blood cells. Folic acid unfortunately stimulated the leukemic blood cells and caused their cancer to quickly progress. After being heavily criticized, Dr. Farber didn't give up but did the opposite. He used drugs that blocked the production of folic acid, and the leukemia improved, the children lived longer and the first chemotherapy was born. Like many inventions, trial and error, missteps and learning from one's mistakes were all part of the process of discovery.

Researchers discovered new chemotherapy drugs. When these powerful drugs were placed into regimens with multiple drugs given in higher doses over longer durations, the success rate of chemotherapy grew. The risks to the patient also grew. As Friedrich Nietzsche said, "That which does not kill us makes us stronger." The most effective chemotherapy protocols now brought patients closer to death in a high stakes trade that hoped for recovery and a life free from cancer. A balancing act developed between the promise of a cure or longer life and the devastating side effects of treatment.

Last fall I had my one chance for a cure. My tongue cancer and surrounding lymph nodes were surgically removed but testing of twenty-six lymph nodes in my neck showed that cancer had already spread into two of them. The cancer appeared aggressive; thus the cancer treatment would need to be equally aggressive. I needed radiation (thirty daily treatments) delivered to my head and neck as well as high-dose chemotherapy with a drug called Cisplatin. To be most effective, the treatments were given at the same time, both with their own unique set of side effects.

When you are receiving a cancer treatment that may cure your cancer, there is a willingness to suffer greatly. By the time I had completed treatment last fall, I had a gastrostomy feeding tube coursing through my abdominal wall into my stomach. My tongue and mouth were covered with painfully large and open sores. I couldn't swallow, and I was on high doses of narcotic pain relievers, and for a couple weeks it was even too painful to talk. I lost fifteen pounds from vomiting and muscle wasting. I felt feverish as my body tried to repair the damage inflicted by my cancer treatment.

During that time, I would sleep fitfully at night thinking that if I didn't wake up, it would be a relief. I have never felt that way before or since. The physical agony was that harsh.

This spring when the cancer returned, I again started on chemotherapy. I take two different chemotherapy drugs, Erbitux and Taxol, but the side effects are much less severe than last fall. Chemotherapy will no longer cure my cancer which has spread into my neck, chest and skin. The chemotherapy is used to improve the pain in my neck and jaw by slowing the growth and progression of my cancer. Without the promise of a possible cure, there is no reason to undergo the same type of aggressive treatment that I endured last fall. I am grateful not to be going through a brutal treatment again.

Cancer patients sometimes have difficult decisions to make. Are the side effects of the treatment worth the opportunity to live longer? How important is the quality of life versus length of life? My cancer is at a stage where I want to live free from significant pain. That is far more important than living longer.

Just like a poker game, we are dealt a hand in life. We may be dealt a good hand or a bad hand. Be careful how you interpret and play your hand. The Bible reminds us over and over that many people who are given a bad hand in life will receive strength to endure and hear God's message of hope for the future. Being dealt a good hand on earth comes with greater responsibility and perhaps a faulty belief that we are self-sufficient, able to make it on our own hard work, and are not in need of God.

I have been dealt a great hand in life. Last fall, in the midst of chemotherapy and radiation, I had a taste of what it feels like to be dealt a bad hand. Unlike poker, in God's world, a bad hand isn't a losing hand. The need for faith in God has never been greater than what I experienced last fall. The cancer treatment didn't kill all of my cancer, but it did send me a reminder that God, and not I, is in control.

***

What kind of hand have you been dealt in life? Or is life a series of hands?

Have you or a loved one needed to make difficult healthcare decisions?

Did you feel supported in those difficult decisions?

Who do you think is in control of your life: God? Yourself? Others around you? All of the above?

19. "My grace is sufficient for you."

October 13, 2014

This past Sunday, our church celebrated St. Luke's Sunday with a healing service. Luke was a physician, and the Gospel of Luke highlights Jesus' compassion toward the ill and the needy. In this healing service, people can choose to come forward to receive a blessing and prayers for healing, anointing with oil and laying on of hands. Not everyone comes forward. I think it is because we associate healing as something that is done only for those who are physically sick. The Bible makes it clear that we are all in need of spiritual healing, which is more important than any physical illness.

Yet we can't help ourselves. When faced with a physical illness or malady, distress and worry tend to consume us. Spiritually, illness and pain can drive us into one of two directions: either closer to or farther from God. We can blame God and bargain for a better life, or we can accept what has happened and ask for God's help in the next step in our life. Even the apostle Paul pleaded with the Lord for healing and was told, "My grace is sufficient for you, for my power is made perfect in weakness" (II Corinthians 12:9).

I have felt blessed by many who have told me that they pray for a miracle, for a cure to my cancer that medical science wouldn't predict or expect. I am grateful and humbled by those prayers and ask that they continue. Yet I have not prayed for God to cure my cancer. I have prayed for pain and nausea relief because it distracts my thoughts and centers them on myself. Instead of asking for a cure, I pray that God's will be done. I don't believe that I will change God's mind but I do know that praying to God changes my heart and mind.

Many believe that I am being cheated in life. I am fifty-seven years old, and not expected to reach seventy-eight, the average life expectancy in the US. God should receive my gratitude for fifty-seven great years of life. I don't believe that God is my ATM, giving me whatever I want or request or granting me special favor on earth that I have not earned or deserved. "My grace is sufficient for you."

Terminal cancer does spontaneously resolve. Although rare and seemingly unpredictable, it does happen. Psychotherapist Kelly Turner wrote her PhD thesis and eventually a book after reviewing 955 cases in which cancer patients experienced an unexpected remission of cancer. She described two nutritional and seven psychological and spiritual factors that seemed to make a difference in this cohort of patients.

Unfortunately, this can fuel the belief that curing widespread cancer is as simple as better nutrition and a hopeful outlook. I have read that 50% of cancer patients given a terminal diagnosis will seriously consider traveling out of the country in search of a cure. There are many practitioners and clinics in Mexico, South and Central America, and worldwide that advertise curing thousands of patients with cancer. Over the years, I saw a number of cancer patients who ventured out of the country at the end of life, only to see their hopes for a cure dashed. They often ended up guiltily blaming themselves for not having enough faith or discipline to be cured of their cancer. I have traveled enough in the world to distrust many of these self-proclaimed health gurus with curative powers, understanding that the desire to make money from any situation is still alive and well throughout the world. Yet I readily acknowledge that there is much that we do not understand about our bodies' intrinsic ability to heal.

So what about God? Can God cure my cancer? Absolutely. Will God cure my cancer? That's God's call, not mine. "Ask and you shall receive" doesn't mean that God gives us all that we desire. A good parent would never give a child anything he wants. Pain and illness has a purpose. I am a more compassionate person today than I was before experiencing the trials of cancer and its treatment. I have never felt freer to share my faith than when I realized that the end of life is nearing. A miraculous cure would have robbed me of some of life's greatest lessons.

In the meantime, I rejoice at the response I've had to five months of palliative chemotherapy (to relieve symptoms). Studies would suggest that on average I would live an extra several months by taking my current chemotherapy weekly. I tolerate taking it only every three weeks and still have experienced positive results beyond expectations.

I feel much better today than I did in May of this year when my cancer had rapidly spread and when I received the news that my cancer was now terminal. I am on much less pain medication. My cancer has regressed as evidenced by improved pain, less swelling (lymphedema) in my neck, easier swallowing, and no further skin metastases. I could never fully appreciate how good I feel today, had I not traversed a valley of pain.

Symptoms like pain can't be placed on the back burner. I am blessed with less pain and a better quality of life than I had ever imagined in May. While I don't consider myself cured, this is an answer to prayer. Without ongoing pain, it is easier to listen to the words of the Lord's Prayer, "Thy will be done, on earth as it is in heaven," and to accept what is ahead, giving thanks for what is behind.

***

Has misfortune driven you closer to or farther away from God?

For what purpose do people experience pain?

Can one truly appreciate wellness without having illness?

20. Norm projects

October 21, 2014

I grew up in a family that liked to build. My dad's name is Norm, and my friends sometimes referred to our building projects as "Norm projects." Our family eventually built two cabins, a garage, an addition onto our house and a road through the woods by our cabin. Additional building projects were completed later in life. My father is eighty-five years old and still delights in learning new woodworking techniques alongside three other men who share their tools in a woodshop. My dad is the youngster in that group: living proof that we should never set aside the joy of learning and creating.

Growing up, my dad was instigator, architect, general contractor, subcontractor and general laborer on these building projects. My mom played the important supporting role of chef as well as being in charge of all cleaning services and paint projects. A week of vacation in our family might be a week of construction. My father never told us why we built as much as we did, but I believe it had something to do with my dad being a farm boy who found himself transplanted into suburban Minneapolis.

When I was growing up, I don't recall my parents ever encouraging us to choose any particular occupation, with one exception: farming. My parents both grew up on farms. They raised their family in Fridley, a suburb of Minneapolis. I have no doubt that they feared raising "city kids" who wouldn't respect the work and effort of farmers.

When I was in high school, my two brothers and I helped him to build a road up by our cabin. We would spend all day with chain saws, axes and splitting mauls, taking down trees and chopping firewood. My older brother Dan once asked my dad if we could buy a wood splitter. As his three boys looked intently at him for his answer, he replied, "I already have three wood splitters." Even though all of his children entered white collar professions, my parents made sure that we knew how it felt to do physical work for an entire day. We learned to respect the work done by farmers or any other worker who puts in long, hard days doing physical labor.

Perhaps the real genius behind my parents' work projects was that they knew how to make the work rewarding and enjoyable. We didn't mind working from sunup to sundown in the woods or while building a cabin. When building the road, I prodded my dad to allow me to occasionally miss a day of school to work in the woods. It seemed cool and a little mischievous. He knew that I was a good student and wouldn't suffer academically by taking a day off. My father did say, that "The most important lessons in life occur outside of the classroom."

My parents figured out that a day of hard work was sweetened by candy bars and ice cream. The only time we ever stopped for ice cream was on the way home from working on the cabin. We received candy bars only when it was an afternoon break during a full day of physical work. At the end of the day, my father always paused and had us look back to see what we had accomplished that day. If work ethic is what my parents wanted to instill in us, they mastered the formula.

The summer after my high school graduation, my parents decided to add a family room onto our house with a woodshop in the basement (which was no less important than the family room). I would work all morning on the addition, often side by side with my dad. In the afternoons I would take a city bus downtown to a monotonous office summer job. The morning construction work was much more fun and interesting. There were many days when I wanted to keep building on our house instead of hopping the bus to punch the clock downtown.

My dad was a natural instructor. We didn't just build. He would explain the rationale for how a building is constructed. We typically discussed construction options, and he allowed his children to help make decisions. He shared advice like "measure twice, cut once" or anecdotes about building projects gone awry. Usually it involved someone who decided a square, level, chalk line or other tool wasn't necessary equipment in their construction project. He learned construction by reading and asking a lot of questions but ultimately knew that natural consequences were the greatest instructor of all. Natural consequences (the problems created by not doing something right the first time) were not just an instructor in building projects but were an instructor in life.

My dad was resourceful and frugal. When a tornado hit Fridley and he suddenly had access to free building materials, he built a cabin. When he found fantastic deals on a window close-out sale and cedar siding, he built a second cabin in the Black Hills of South Dakota. He didn't like throwing things away and found uses for building materials that might have otherwise ended up in a dumpster.

I think the most important lesson I learned was that physical work and construction is a welcome respite from a white collar job. My father loved being a parish pastor and Lutheran bishop, and I loved being a family physician. But we both were employed in sedentary jobs that work the mind but not the body. We learned the joy of sweating, exerting, creating and seeing the visible results of a hard day's work. Sore muscles at the end of the day weren't painful; instead they were a palpable sign of a job well done.

***

What memories of parenting techniques do?

What are some of the most important lessons learned growing up that were learned outside of the classroom?

How does working together build relationships?

21. Life of crime - Narrowly averted?

October 29, 2014

Last weekend, Amy and I visited Liz and Jay Vogt in Pierre, SD. Liz is my cousin, and because we were the same age and liked fun and adventure, we were close growing up, even though we lived 250 miles apart. "You need to watch those two," my grandmother sternly warned our parents, "because they are going to be trouble."

I was only eight years old when three tornadoes hit my hometown of Fridley, MN. As you might imagine, household items were strewn into the yards and onto the streets. The morning after the tornado, I stepped on a nail. A nurse friend came over and cleaned out the puncture wound, wrapping my foot in a thick gauze bandage. I was homebound.

All the neighbor kids plundered the streets and yards for hidden treasures. Several times each day they would parade into our house where I was marooned with my foot injury. They showed me all of the cool stuff they were finding. I know my parents wouldn't have approved of me pilfering all of those things. It might have been just as well that I was left hopping around the house on one foot. I never got the chance to steal anything. Life of crime – narrowly averted.

The neighborhood kids liked to throw snowballs or garden tomatoes (whichever was in season) at cars. We were never more thrilled than when the driver got out of his car and with an adrenaline rush, the chase was on. We made the mistake one time of throwing at our neighbor's car. It was a snazzy Cadillac, and he treated it like it was a prized member of the family. He quickly drove home and realized that his own boys weren't home. His sons got in trouble, but the rest of us escaped punishment. It did stop us from pegging defenseless cars with snowballs or tomatoes. Life of crime – narrowly averted.

While running cross country in high school, my favorite summer running route was a five-mile loop that ended at a swimming pool store. My teammates and I would climb a chain-linked fence to gain access, and enjoyed cooling off after our run. The pool store was adjacent to a busy road so initially we were cautious, kept our heads low, and tried to stay out of sight in a covered pool. It didn't take long before we were boldly sliding down the slides, throwing tennis balls back and forth, and making a lot of waves and noise. I probably did this twenty times with some cross country teammates. The one time I didn't go, the police showed up. My friends had to jump the fence and run barefoot through the woods to escape the police. After the bust, we never ventured back to the pool store again. Life of crime - narrowly averted.

In high school, we sometimes would TP (toilet paper) a yard. One of our friends happened to be the superintendent's son. When some friends of mine decided to TP his yard, I declined. Even though I knew it wasn't directed toward the superintendent, I correctly surmised that nothing good could happen from selecting this particular target. Sure enough, my friends ended up in detention after school. Life of crime – narrowly averted.

I turned eighteen years of age on April 23 with just weeks left in my senior year of high school. A new school rule determined that as an adult, an 18 year old could sign notes releasing themselves from school. I started handing in notes to the high school secretary, stating that I had an appointment with Dr. Greenhaven. Greenhaven was a local golf course, and a group of us eighteen-year-olds would skip school to go golfing. I was soon called into the principal's office. He said, "David, in one week you are going to be named valedictorian of your class. You should be the picture of academic excellence. For God's sake, would you please just show up for class?" I quit having appointments with Dr. Greenhaven. Life of crime – narrowly averted.

I have fond memories of growing up and seeing my own children grow up. I didn't really narrowly avert a life of crime. Like many teenagers, I was emboldened by being in a group of friends and liked taking a few risks to have some fun and adventure. It is by the grace of God that most children grow up eventually learning to do the right thing. My behavior did change. Some people live and learn; others just live.

Our children also didn't narrowly avert a life a crime as far as I know. Then again, most of my stories were never told to my parents until much later in life. Many parents of teenagers can state that "Our children are doing some interesting things, many of which we are unaware." Maybe it's time to grill our two sons for a few stories. As my friend Dan Wood says with a laugh, "The only good thing about a bad decision is the story that comes out of it."

***

Can you recall some times when you got into trouble or narrowly averted trouble growing up?

Were you an easy or difficult teenager to raise?

Do you tend to live and learn, or just live?

22. An unforgettable day

November 5, 2014

Many cancer patients are propelled through a roller-coaster-like ride as they deal with treatments, side-effects, and an altered life after a diagnosis of cancer. There is no controlling the ups and down, twists and turns of a track that is invisible and scary.

This past Sunday was an unforgettable day for me. I ran the Rails to Trails Marathon on the Elroy-Sparta Bike Trail in Wisconsin with a group of friends. A few weeks ago, I took my first run in many months. Two weeks later, I completed a 13-mile training run. I decided to enter a marathon before the snow flies and before the prospect of running a Wisconsin marathon is frozen beyond the realm of possibility.

I tried to run a couple times in June of this year. It didn't go well. My legs were weak, and I tired quickly. I had shed thirty pounds, mostly muscle. My previously skin-tight bike shorts hung loosely over my skin. I was convinced that I would never run again and certainly never run a marathon.

I was so sure that my running days were over that I retired my lifetime entry at Grandma's Marathon: Not a bad investment considering that I had run 25 Grandma's Marathons off a $100 lifetime entry purchased in 1980. I also gave away my favorite pair of cushioned running shoes to my friend Fritz since we share the same shoe size and he was having some foot pain. He offered to return them when I started running again, but I assured him that I have never experienced a drought when it comes to having enough running shoes on hand.

Slowly but surely, my body has experienced a remarkable rejuvenation since this past summer. I am gaining weight, te is back, and the strength in my legs is unexpected but greatly appreciated.

I have never run a marathon where I needed to walk. But I started the Rails to Trails Marathon with a short walk every two miles to ensure that I had enough energy left to finish the race. A big bonus: four other running friends signed on for the adventure - Terry Sullivan, Lisa Buhr, Gary Hoffman and Greg Kleindl. I wore a headlamp to light our way through the old ¾-mile train tunnel on the Elroy-Sparta Trail. We joked that the headlamp might be needed to see the finish line at the end of the race if we finished after dusk.

It wasn't an easy run for me but I was thrilled to finish in 4 hours and 54 minutes. I have run ninety marathons, and this one was by far the slowest. Yet it is the most memorable marathon that I have ever run. In many respects, it felt like I was running a marathon for the first time with my regenerated body and a group of friends urging me on to the finish line.

As children, we dream about the big and great things that we can accomplish. It is very self-centered. As we grow older, we are able to move beyond our own dreams and goals to helping others achieve theirs. Helping others to live out their dreams and reach their goals is among the greatest joys of life. We are successful when we contribute to the success of others.

The special part of Sunday's marathon was that my running friends hung back with me to be a mobile crowd of cheerleaders helping me get to the finish line. The constant chatter and banter that has always been a part of my running community accompanied me from start to finish. It was emotional for me. It was more than the already exceptional reality that my body had recovered to the point where it can once again complete a marathon. It was special that, with very short notice, four friends changed their plans and signed up to run with me.

The Bible states, "Love your neighbor as yourself" as the second greatest commandment (Matt. 22:39) and, "Do unto others as you would have them do unto you," which was coined the Golden Rule (Matt. 7:12). When we think about who in our lives represents the Golden Rule, we come up with our best friends, our favorite work colleagues, our spouses, and families, and I will include my running partners. I have been privileged in life to be surrounded by incredibly caring people who will willingly put my needs and desires ahead of theirs.

I don't know when or if I will ever run another marathon. I do know this: Living with cancer has been a roller coaster ride, and I'm not steering the ride or operating the throttle. I will no longer assume that anything from running marathons to returning to meaningful work is out of the realm of possibility. God, and not I, is in control.

Sunday, I felt like I was at the top of the roller coaster climb. It would be nice if I can pause there for a while. I am thankful to the runners who spurred me on to the finish line to attain a goal that wasn't on my radar months ago. They gifted me an unforgettable day.

Thanks.

***

Have you had the chance to contribute to the success of others or help them attain a goal?

Have family or friends ever gifted you an unforgettable day? What did you do?

Have you ever done something that you thought was impossible?

23. Clown hair

November 12, 2014

I recently saw my longtime barber Dave Kregness for a haircut. His barbershop is called Dave's Golden Shears. When our kids were young, they thought Goldenshears was his last name, and I would simply tell them that I was having my ears lowered by Mr. Goldenshears.

After a greeting, Dave always asks, "Do you want it cut the same?" He has cut my hair the same way and to the same length for twenty-seven years so there isn't much to discuss. This last time, however, I told him what chemotherapy was doing to my hair. It is clearly thinning from the chemotherapy. More noticeable is the frizzing and curling that occurs around the temples. I hadn't been to him in a long time because with all the frizziness, I was unsure if I needed a haircut.

"I can fix that," Dave said when he looked at me. "It looks like clown hair, and if I trim it short, your hair will look more normal again." Far be it from me to be seen wandering around town looking like a clown. Of course, none of my chemo treatments caused me to lose all of my hair. In that scenario, I could have worn a wig to hide my baldness. It is interesting how important it becomes for us not to look different from everyone else.

When I was initially placed on chemotherapy last fall, my friend Ted Bensen assumed that I would lose all of my hair. He proudly announced that he would be honored to lead the charge to have some other men shave their heads, so I wouldn't feel alone. It turns out that Ted has been balding for years and already shaves his head so it wasn't going to be a big sacrifice for him. It was good for a laugh.

Many of us have physical imperfections. I was born with severely crossed eyes (strabismus) because of a lazy eye (amblyopia). I had strabismus surgery at age two to correct the crossed eyes. It was partially successful. My right eye still wanders to the right, and so I always have one eye looking at you and one looking over your left shoulder. I never developed normal 3-dimensional vision and regularly fail depth perception tests.

I never regarded this as a handicap. Since I have never known normal depth perception, I haven't missed it. Sometimes people comment that my eyes aren't straight or ask what I'm looking at or even look over their left shoulder to see what my right eye might be focusing on. Never knowing any other life, I am not embarrassed or dismayed by it.

When I became a physician, I became aware that I could have another operation on my eyes to realign the lazy eye and put it in line with my other more dominant eye. It wouldn't help my vision or depth perception. Essentially it would be cosmetic surgery.

I never considered the operation. I am fully accepting of my eyes. I have lived with them my entire life and don't feel disabled by them except when pheasant hunting (the birds are safe, but the other hunters need to take cover). Some would argue that I could make a better first impression when meeting others if my eyes were aligned. Yet I wouldn't undertake any level of surgical risk just to attempt to align my two eyes when there is nothing functional to gain.

Not all physical imperfections are bad. It is interesting that one of my chemotherapy meds (Erbitux) causes acne, and people who develop significant acne have a better result. I broke out with acne over my chest, back and face. I have never been so delighted in my life to get zits.

Many people spend considerable time, energy and money on personal appearance. I read a study in which fifty adults and children were asked, "If you could change one thing about your body, what would it be?" Without hesitation, the adults chose a physical "flaw" they wanted to change. The children, on the other hand, struggled to find anything they wanted to change. Instead, they wished for superhuman additions. Children felt comfortable in their own skin. We as adults could learn from them.

Although many of my patients want to lose weight, I found that we often had different reasons for desiring to be more slender. I wanted patients to be healthy and fit through a balanced diet and regular exercise. Many patients wanted to "look better." When substantial weight loss occurred, inevitably patients would remark that they felt so much more energetic. They transitioned from desiring to lose weight just so they could look better to wanting to lose weight so they could feel better.

I want to feel better. Personal appearance has become a low priority. I don't try to get the gray or frizz out of my hair or wear cover-up on my acne or massage the lymphedema out of my neck. Having a beautiful physical appearance isn't on the bucket list of most people living with cancer and approaching the end of life. Life is about relationships that don't require me to look good to maintain them.

I don't know when I will have my next haircut, but the clown hair is rather unique. I will probably have fewer haircuts in the future and accept a hairstyle that is used by clowns to make people laugh.

***

How important is your personal, physical appearance to you?

If you could change one thing about your appearance, would you do it? What would you change?

If you lost all your hair because of chemotherapy, would you wear a wig, to boldly (or baldly) proclaim your cancer treatment side-effects?

24. Rural family medicine

November 19, 2014

This past Saturday, I attended the Wisconsin Academy of Family Physicians (WAFP) Board of Directors meeting in Green Lake, Wisconsin. I was elected president of the organization and served in that capacity from February to May of this year before my progressive cancer forced my resignation. One of the endearing qualities of the WAFP is that it isn't just a trade organization that advocates for family physicians. It has more noble goals, seeking to improve the health and healthcare for the people of Wisconsin.

I was asked to attend the meeting to further discuss an award that the WAFP Foundation had proposed and will manage: the David C. Eitrheim, MD Rural Resident Scholarship. I thought I was going to be asked to supply more input and was instead ambushed by a very nice presentation of the new scholarship award. A dedicated endowment will fund the award. I stood in front of the board of directors as some members pledged money to start the endowment. It was a very kind ambush – a pleasant surprise that left me feeling humbled by their generosity.

They loaded me up with several nice gifts including a plaque that outlined the description and process related to the award and includes the following: "The David C. Eitrheim, MD Rural Resident Scholarship award will be given annually beginning in 2015 to a first year resident in a Wisconsin residency program that demonstrates an interest and commitment to rural family medicine. The purpose of the award is to help offset expenses incurred with rural rotations and to fund attendance at the American Academy of Family Physicians Annual Assembly."

I am a fan of rural family medicine. Although I practiced in a community that is too large for me to call myself a true rural family physician, I did serve as director of the Menomonie Family Medicine Rural Training Track Residency program. Our program was designed to train medical residents in the full scope of family medicine so that they would be comfortable practicing in small rural communities that pepper our state. Just like our faculty family physicians and me, they became comfortable with the entire range of family medicine: not just seeing patients in clinic visits, but delivering babies, caring for hospitalized and nursing home patients, working ER shifts, and performing minor surgical procedures.

We trained four family medicine residents in Menomonie before we closed the program in 2003. I'm delighted that three of the four graduates still are my colleagues in Menomonie and Glenwood City. I would gladly have any of them as our family's family physician.

We closed the residency program when the number of US medical school graduates choosing family medicine dropped by 50%. It became increasingly difficult to recruit high quality US-trained medical students to our program. I worked with many medical students throughout my career and can tell you that it has become increasingly more difficult to convince students that family medicine should be their career choice.

There is plenty of data showing that the United States would benefit by encouraging more physicians (and physician assistants and nurse practitioners) to enter primary care. Americans spend much more than any other developed country on health care. Yet they don't receive the results that should correlate to this high price tag. Medicare data shows that areas of the country with the highest proportion of primary care physicians have lower costs and better health outcomes than areas with a low proportion of primary care physicians. Unfortunately the number of medical students choosing a primary care specialty (family medicine, general internal medicine, geriatrics or pediatrics) is in sharp decline. Distribution of physicians is an additional problem with a dismally low number of new physicians choosing to locate in a rural area (only 4.8%).

I am pleased that the WAFP Foundation has developed a scholarship that helps financially but also honors the work and commitment of rural family physicians. One of my heroes is Dr. Frank Springer. Frank is ninety-one years old and continued to see nursing home patients until age ninety. His love of medicine, his care for patients, his engaging life stories and commitment to the community of Elmwood, WI, over his lifetime is admirable. The summer after Frank completed his medical training, he returned to his hometown of Elmwood for a summer break. The aging lone physician in Elmwood called in sick one day, and Frank came in to see patients for him. That physician never returned to work, and Frank never left. Those two physicians served the town of Elmwood for over ninety years. Very few small towns are that fortunate.

Our rural areas need more family physicians like Frank Springer. My hope is that this scholarship will be a way of thanking a family medicine resident who will infuse their time, energy and life into a rural Wisconsin community.

***

Do you have a family physician or other primary care provider that you know and trust for your medical care?

What are the advantages/disadvantages to receiving care from a family doctor, verses a specialist?

25. Grounded in gratitude or, glass half empty or half full?

November 26, 2014

By Amy Jo Eitrheim

Many years ago, our family was invited to the birthday party of a five-year-old. She was an only child. We arrived at the surprise party with gift in hand. I searched for a spot on the dining room table on which to place the gift, which was already piled high and overflowing with colorfully wrapped presents. I carefully slid our gift onto the table and was worried that other gifts would fall off the crammed table.

When the guest of honor burst into the room, we all shouted "Surprise!" She looked around at all of us and at the gifts and blurted out, "Where are the rest of my presents?" I quickly clamped my hand over my mouth to stifle a cry/laugh of disbelief and shock. Was she kidding? The REST of her presents?

Many of you ask how I am doing with Dave's cancer, and many of you tell us you are praying for me and our boys, as well as for Dave. Thank you very much. It means a lot to me to have this support and to know you care about us. We are so grateful for your letters and cards, entries on CaringBridge, and personal visits. We live in a great community and feel your love in many ways.

I am doing all right. I strive to take one day at a time and to focus my energy on being positive. I try to stay in the moment and not let my thoughts drift too far into the future. I try to help Dave have good days: less suck/more awesome. Instead of self-pity, I remind myself of how lucky I am to be partnered with this extraordinary man and to count the many blessings of my life. We have been happily married for thirty-two years; we have two wonderful sons who are the pride and joy of our lives; we have enjoyed good health; we each grew up in loving, Christian families; we were able to take advantage of education and to contribute in careers which help others. I could go on and on...

I read a book entitled "Living life as a thank you- The Transformative Power of Daily Gratitude" by Nina Lesowitz and Mary Beth Sammons. In it the authors offer a simple approach for incorporating gratitude into daily life. Each chapter relates stories of people whose lives had been changed by the powerful acknowledgement of the blessings in their lives. I will share one quote: "Gratitude is the intention to count your blessings every day, every minute, while avoiding, whenever possible, the belief that you need or deserve different circumstances."

To somehow feel cheated in life is to be like that indulged five-year old: ignoring the mountain of gifts and wondering why there aren't more presents. It feels wrong to me, to complain about a future that may not follow my expectations, all the while being showered with countless blessings I do not deserve. If I remain grounded in gratitude, I can focus on all of God's goodness and grace. Gratitude is my prayer. My glass is half full. No. Overflowing.

Thanks be to God.

P.S. Happy Thanksgiving!

***

What is the harm in 'spoiling' our kids?

How does a strong sense of gratitude develop in children?

26. Acceptance

December 3, 2014

In the 1969 book, <u>On Death and Dying</u>, Elisabeth Kübler-Ross described five stages of grief, a series of emotional stages when faced with impending death. The five stages are denial, anger, bargaining, depression and acceptance. She asserted that grievers may travel through some or all of the five stages of grief – in any order and sometimes at the same time.

From the first day of my diagnosis of tongue cancer in July of 2013, my stage of grief has resided in acceptance. I don't deny that I am terminally ill. I'm not angry that cancer came into my life. I'm not bargaining with God to receive a miraculous cure. I haven't felt depressed by my lot in life. I live in acceptance.

I am not insightful enough to know exactly why I am so accepting of having a cancer diagnosis or terminal illness. I know that my life as a family physician has taught me to accept the inevitability of death. I have admired those who approached their death with courage and grace. I am sure that my Christian faith and belief in heaven helps me to accept death. Death isn't the end of life, but the beginning of a life with God that is devoid of the suffering and angst of earthly life.

I have enjoyed an exceptionally good response to my current chemotherapy. If I lied and told you that I am fighting this cancer with all my strength, many of you would praise me. You might be in awe of my exceptional fortitude or my unabashed will to live. We revel in our beliefs that it is our own willpower that creates great results.

I'm living with great results but it's not my own doing. My chemotherapy is fighting my cancer. If I have to battle anything, it is against the side effects of my chemo. We are resilient people but still give ourselves too much credit for our body's response to cancer treatments. It isn't my willpower that has done this.

If I credit myself for good results, then I set myself up as a failure when cancer eventually consumes my health and forges onward to death. It elevates my highs and depresses the lows of living with a terminal illness. Crediting ourselves confirms our poor understanding of God. If we really understood heaven, we would embrace death and treasure the inevitability of a future with God. If we really understood prayer, we would focus on praising God for all of the healing and goodness that has entered our lives. If we really understood God, we would be in awe daily of everything around us, on earth and in heaven. We would trust God in all our endeavors and credit God for the blessings of life.

Studies have shown that people with a strong will to live tend to live longer. I believe that this is true primarily because people who are more ill lose their will to live. I have a stronger will to live now than I did in May of this year when I was awakening throughout the night needing another dose of morphine to ease my pain and allow sleep. My cancer was rapidly progressing and painful in May. Many cancer patients in this situation begin to see death as a release from suffering. People around us shouldn't take it as a personal affront when their loved one loses the will to live. Instead it is time to find out what your loved one wants at the end of life. Don't be surprised if relief of pain and other symptoms from their rapidly progressive cancer are at the top of the list.

Families struggle when a loved one loses the will to live at the end of life. They take it personally. People are resilient. We don't lose our desire to live a longer life with our spouse, to see our children grow older and to reach the next stage of life, or to help our parents at the end of their lives. Yet many cancer patients are overwhelmed by pain, narcotic side effects, weakness and dependence at the end of life. Their desire to live a longer life with their families didn't end, but the ability to enjoy life faded away.

There is a selfish part of me that wants to take some credit for my improvement these past months. I can say that I have remained physically fit throughout my life and that cancer patients who are physically fit do tend to live longer. Yet I am far too accepting of my cancer to believe that I willed any of this to happen. I thank God for the unexpected great result. I am a hyper-responder to my chemotherapy, and I have no problem believing that God works through my chemo to bring comfort and healing, even if it won't continue forever.

Acceptance is good. When we accept that we can't fight and win, we can prepare for death. I am dying, and so are you. We should all be prepared for it. There is no reason to approach the end of life expecting results that aren't going to happen.

I have already had important conversations with Amy and our sons about my wishes at the end of life. I want to be comfortable, and I don't want life unnecessarily extended. I live in acceptance. I am resilient, but I don't plan on fighting to the end when it becomes clear that death is no longer the enemy but has become the friend. This isn't a battle. God can call me home when it is time. At life's end, I won't be trying one last futile therapy to extend that time by a few days or weeks. In the meantime, I will enjoy an improvement in health that isn't my own doing, accepting the past as well as the future.

***

How would you describe your current state of health?

Have you seen a loved one lose the will to live? Did you take it personally as a sign of rejection?

Do you know of someone who has died but wouldn't accept that death was approaching? How was this handled?

How can a dying person make it easier for others around them to accept death?

If death comes to every one of us, why is the death of each person we love so painful? How can this strengthen our relationships?

27. Humbled in Haiti

December 9, 2014

I skipped my medical school graduation ceremony as did my good friend Mark Deyo-Svendsen. Instead we embarked on a month-long mission trip to Haiti with our wives.

It was an eye-opening experience as Haiti is the poorest country in the Western Hemisphere. We worked in an orphanage, laid concrete blocks to build a hospital and held some medical clinics. The experience made us all the more thankful for our easy, comfortable lives in the US.

We were into the last days of our trip. Heading to Port au Prince, the capital city, we would soon catch a flight back to the US. Riding in an old rickety pickup truck, some of us were bouncing around in the pickup truck bed as we rode down a winding dirt road through the mountains.

Without warning, our truck suddenly veered sharply to the left and slammed into the mountainside. Although we were thrown around in the bed of the pickup, no one was hurt. We hopped out and surveyed the damage. The rear axle had broken. Eventually our eyes shifted from the axle to the road. Our truck had veered left. Looking to the right, we saw the downhill slope of the mountain. It was a steep ravine. Had our truck veered right, it was a sobering thought that serious injuries or death likely would have been the end result.

We didn't have a lot of time to ponder our good fortune. It was evening, the darkness was stark, and it was raining hard. We wandered down the muddy road that had almost led to our demise, stopping at a lone single-room hut on the side of the road. Our interpreter, speaking in Creole, introduced us to a family working feverishly to take advantage of the downpour.

We stepped inside the tiny hut for cover from the rain. The mother of the household had released a small earthen dam outside the hut to allow a trickling stream of water to course through their hut. She was busy mixing a clay-like mud in the center of the floor. Her husband was slapping handfuls of it against their walls which were made from sticks bound together by grass. They were building the walls of their house. Their smiles were contagious, and they were obviously delighted by the rainstorm. It gave them the building materials needed to complete the construction of their home.

Meanwhile, we met one of their sons. He smiled broadly as he proudly displayed his role in the family project. He held the light source. His light was simple. It was a large bottle cap, filled with oil and illuminated by the flame of a single wick. It supplied enough light for mom and dad to work, and he was obviously excited to share the light with all of us.

We pulled out some raisins to share with the family. Their gratitude for a handful of raisins was one of those truly humbling experiences of life. While the family lived in threadbare poverty when it came to possessions, there was no poverty of spirit. They were thrilled to have the rain to build their home. They were obviously pleased by the opportunity to be hospitable to a group of strangers by sharing shelter, light and the warmth of their smiles.

Money does not buy happiness, but giving does. There is research evidence that spending money on ourselves does not make us happy. People who spend money on others do become happier, and research suggests that the value of the gift is not important in determining happiness. Even a very small gift increases happiness. In 2010, a worldwide Gallup poll revealed that there is also a positive correlation between charitable acts, such as helping a stranger, and happiness. This correlation held true in virtually all of the 153 countries surveyed, and many poor countries were high on the list of both charity toward others and happiness. We should not be surprised that an impoverished Haitian family that warmly shared simplest of light and shelter would be a happy f

We did eventually catch a bus to Port au Prince and fle. home. Some memories in life never go away, nor should they. We had walked down a dark mountain road, complaining that we were cold, damp and stranded without transportation. We left charmed by the elation of a poor Haitian family that shared their humble home with us. Anytime that I wonder if I should have more in life, I think back to the sheer joy displayed by that Haitian family. Joy in life does not come from our material wealth. Watching an indigent family that worked together, showed generosity towards strangers, and celebrated a rainstorm so they could make mud was the highlight of that trip.

We should never wait until the end of life to realize how much we have been given in life. We are not rich by what we possess, but by our spirit of love and kindness toward others. A near disaster in Haiti led to a humbling life lesson.

***

What have been your experiences in underdeveloped countries? How did the experiences make you feel about the wealth many Americans enjoy?

What do you think of the statement, "money doesn't buy happiness, but giving does?"

Tell of a time when you were able to share something that was significant for the person who received it.

28. Honoring Choices

December 17, 2014

Our country spends an incredible amount of money trying to extend the lives of terminally ill patients at the end of life. As physicians, we are trained to keep people alive. We are not as proficient at helping people as they die. Regrettably, treatments are sometimes offered to dying patients that have at best only a slim chance of working. Terminally ill patients who die in the hospital undergoing every possible treatment to extend life should have their cases reviewed. Did anyone spend the time to determine what the patient wanted at the end of life? Shame on the medical profession if that conversation didn't occur.

There were many times when I met with a family at the tail end of a loved one's life and already knew what the patient desired based on previous conversations. It allowed me to support the decision to embrace death by providing comfort care and by forgoing treatments that offered only a sliver of hope. Families could accept death without guilt, knowing that their loved one was ready to die and had conveyed that message.

When you are hospitalized, your familiar family doc may no longer be caring for hospital patients. You may have doctors caring for you who don't know you or your family. Fortunately there is a movement towards using palliative care specialists at the end of life. They specialize not just in reducing the uncomfortable symptoms that can surround death but also in ensuring that the critical conversation about what a patient really wants at the end of life occurs. Everyone rests easier when that conversation has taken place.

I find it troubling that physicians die differently than the general population. Doctors with terminal illness are more likely than the general public to forego futile treatments at the end of life. They are less likely to die under the bright fluorescent lights of the ICU or to undergo one last round of chemotherapy that may cause more harm than good. Physicians often choose hospice care earlier. In Dr. Atul Gawande's book, BEING MORTAL, he noted that there are multiple studies showing the benefit of early hospice care, which interestingly seems to extend life instead of hastening death as many might assume. "The lesson seems almost Zen: you live longer only when you stop trying to live longer."

Doctors are more likely to have advanced directives in place and to have a DNR order (DNR-Do Not Resuscitate is being replaced by a more positive term, AND-Allow Natural Death). They know the futility of performing CPR on a patient dying of a terminal illness. It isn't like the TV shows the general public watched, showing revival back to a normal life.

If you don't have an advanced directive on file with your healthcare provider, you should. Forms are available at your clinic or hospital. With advanced directives, patients select a healthcare agent who can make medical decisions if they become incompetent to make their own decisions. The healthcare agent is there to act as a surrogate for their loved one. The question is simple: "If your loved one could make a decision right now about his medical care, what would he want?" We aren't asking what the family wants. We are asking what the patient would want if he could have made the decision.

The Wisconsin Academy of Family Physicians, the Wisconsin State Medical Society, and many other medical organizations have made "Honoring Choices" one of their key initiatives. Honoring Choices is a program set up to encourage end-of-life discussion in families along with filling out advanced directives. It might rescue many families from the struggle and grief associated with end-of-life decisions.

In 1991, La Crosse, WI, began a community-wide program to have conversations among families and a trained

facilitator about wishes at the end of life. Of the pe
La Crosse, 96% have advanced directives at the time
death because of this program. In the last six month
life, La Crosse residents spend half as many days in the
hospital as the national average. The Mayo Clinic Health
System would like to expand this program to other
communities.

We have to ask our loved ones what they want at the end
of life and can't assume that we know the answer. At age
98, Amy's grandmother developed complications following
surgery and spent the next week on a ventilator. Her
sedation was decreased so she could be asked if she
wanted to continue on the ventilator, even though there
was virtually no chance for recovery. Our family was told
that she chose to continue on the vent. Amy and I were
always suspicious that she never fully understood her
situation. She was groggy from medication and very
weak. Unfortunately, our family did not have the
conversation prior to her illness to really know her desires.
Three days later, with our family still in turmoil over trying
to understand her true wishes, her breathing tube was
removed. She died within fifteen minutes with her family
at her bedside, but she had struggled on a ventilator
through the final ten days of life.

As the holidays approach, you may be getting together
with your family. Talking about death is taboo in many
families. We are reluctant to use holiday time to discuss
end-of-life wishes or advanced directives. Yet it is an
important discussion that may save your family from grief
and guilt and save you from undergoing futile treatments
at the end of life. It is a good way to say, "I love you." A
good resource for opening the discussion is
www.HonoringChoices.org. Best wishes to you and
your family.

***

Why do you think that doctors die differently than the general population?

Physicians tend to apply the brakes to any medical care that may be futile at the end of life. Why do you think doctors may suggest care to a terminally ill patient that they would not want for themselves?

Do you and your family members have advance directives for health care at the end of life? If not, why not?

If you have an advance directive, have you discussed your preferences or thought about end-of-life care with your chosen health care agent, or other family members?

What problems might ensue if you can't communicate your medical decisions at the end of your life, especially if those closest to you are uncertain about your values and wishes?

How can we balance expertise and the uncontrollable to create kindness at life's end?

29. Christmas cheer

December 24, 2014

Last night, the Buhr family (Audric & Lisa) in Menomonie loaded their four children (Tyler, Halle, Carson and Maxwell) into the family car for one of their annual Christmas traditions. They scour the neighborhoods of Menomonie looking for the finest Christmas lights and outdoor holiday display in the area.

While that may not sound unusual, this is more than a mere voyeuristic trip to scope out some lights and reindeer. If your home is honored with the "Outstanding Exterior Holiday Display Award 2014 as voted by the Buhr Family," the fun has only begun. In case your family is slow to warm up to the idea that six strangers have just appeared at your doorstep, the musical Buhr family will carol, "We Wish You a Merry Christmas." You are then awarded with an original one-of-a-kind certificate, bordered by Christmas lights and signed by all six members of the Buhr family. Included is the inscription, "This is in recognition of your phenomenal display of Holiday Cheer. Thank you for sharing your public enthusiasm for the Christmas season."

The Buhr family doesn't stop there. They come carrying gifts of hot cocoa mix, candy canes and a Christmas music CD. If the Buhr family appears at your door on December 23, I urge you to resist calling the police to report suspicious activity outside your house, and instead welcome them into your home to spread some holiday cheer.

Christmas traditions like this are a great way to build lifelong memories, strengthen family bonds, and brighten the holiday season. One of my favorite holiday traditions is the simple sending and receiving of Christmas cards and letters. For those who are interested, I will update you on our family.

Our oldest son Nathan works as a mechanical engineer in Houston, TX. He has applied to grad school which he plans to attend next fall. He hunts and competes in shooting competitions for fun.

Our youngest son Eric is in a PhD chemistry program at the University of Iowa. He will be marrying Sarah Czechowicz in May. We could not be happier for them. Both boys travelled home to spend time with us. It was great seeing them so often.

My cancer returned in May, but I have been blessed with more time and better health than I ever thought would be possible. I retired from clinic practice as a family physician after twenty-seven years. I receive palliative chemotherapy every three weeks. I ran a marathon this fall and continue to get stronger.

My wife Amy is grateful for family and friends. She is working and riding her horse minimally. We have spent more time together than at any other time in our busy lives, and it has been a true joy. We are amazed by the outpouring of love and support from our community. While we have many things to think about, we have nothing to worry about. God is good.

Merry Christmas and God's blessings to you and your family.

***

What Christmas or other holiday traditions provide special meaning or joy for you?

How do you like to be updated on what is going on in the lives of extended family and friends?

What does it mean to say, "While we have many things to think about, we have nothing to worry about?"

30. Miracles: Living in awe of the supernatural

December 31, 2014

We want God to do sensational miraculous healing. I would like to be free of cancer. If that were all that happened, however, I still could be disappointed. I may still have to live with my dry mouth, with the necrotic sore in my mouth that won't heal, and with the radiation-damaged jaw bone and neck muscles that would remain as a constant source of pain and irritation. We have insatiable appetites for living a perfect life.

Instead, we should give thanks to God for all of the healing that we take for granted but is no less miraculous. My chemotherapy causes any cut or sore to heal very slowly. For the first time in my life, I can't assume that something as simple as a crack in my chemo-induced dry skin will heal. There is an amazing number of currently known chemical reactions that must take place flawlessly to allow blood to clot and scar tissue to form when a cut heals. Yet we can wince at having a painful paper cut on a finger and then never think twice about it. We are supremely confident that it will heal. We don't feel a need to pray for it to heal or to give thanks when it does heal. We want to pray instead for big, splashy dramatic miracles of healing yet fail to appreciate all the miracles around us that are part of everyday life.

As a Lutheran bishop, my father had the opportunity to travel to Europe and meet with other European church leaders. The agenda included a private audience with Pope John Paul II. The Pope made a number of interesting comments to that group of Lutheran leaders. One comment really struck me: The pope said, "When I think of America, I see a country that has lost its sense of awe in the supernatural."

It's true. When we believe that an event is explainable through science, it is no longer miraculous. There are now scientific explanations that attempt to explain everything from the Old Testament ten plagues of Egypt, to Moses and the Israelites crossing the Red Sea, to the revelation that the Star of Bethlehem may have simply been the unusual juxtaposition of three bright planets in the same vicinity. As medical and scientific breakthroughs lead to a better understanding of our bodies and of the world, it should not diminish what we believe about God.

Intelligent people aren't wowed by how much we know. They are wowed by how little we know. Inquiring minds and good research should always lead to more questions than answers. Our human minds can't comprehend many things. For example, how can space or time continue into infinity? We really can't comprehend a concept like infinity.

Why am I doing so well in spite of my cancer? Is it a "miracle"? Is it the combined power of many prayers? Is it explained by science?

It probably is explained by science. Erbitux is a chemotherapy that attacks epidermal growth factor receptors that reside on head and neck cancer cells. If you break out with acne, it is a sign that you likely have many of these receptors and that the chemotherapy will be more effective. My back, chest and facial acne are living evidence that I likely have many receptors being attacked by my chemotherapy.

Does this mean that my improvement isn't a miracle and isn't an answer to our prayers and that God doesn't deserve any credit for my improvement? If our answer is "yes," then we have truly lost our sense of awe in the supernatural. God can work through chemotherapy, and it doesn't make my improvement in health any less divine or appreciated. Half of the patients who have recurrent and advanced head and neck cancers don't respond at all to my kind of chemotherapy. Their cancer continues to grow unchecked. If I had been in that group, would it mean that

God didn't answer our prayers? No. The answer to our prayers would have been different. Whether a person's health declines quickly or slowly, God can still cause good things to occur in the time that we have left on earth.

It is time for us to redefine miracles. Perhaps the best evidence that God exists is a simple look around us at His world. It is far too amazing to believe that this happened by chance. To believe that there is no grand architect who engineered all of this is absurd. Just because we have scientific advancements that explain more of the world around us, we should never lose our sense of awe in the supernatural. Our entire world and life is one big supernatural miracle.

***

Where can you see evidence of supernatural forces at work in the world?

As scientists discover more and more, does this diminish or enhance your faith in God? Examples?

What do you think of the last sentence "our entire world and life is one big supernatural miracle?"

31. Alec Johnson: A remarkable life

January 7, 2015

On December 27, Amy and I attended the funeral for forty-year old Alec Johnson, son of our friends Dan and Izzie Johnson. The Johnson family was enjoying a holiday vacation at Bluefin Bay in Tofte, Minnesota, when the unthinkable happened. Alec, standing on the bouldered shore of Lake Superior, was knocked off a rock by a six-foot wave. A sixty-six-year-old passerby attempted to save him and was also swept out to deeper water. Both men drowned in the icy waters of Lake Superior as rescue attempts by family members and first responders were unsuccessful.

It is admirable that a Good Samaritan gave his life in an attempt to rescue Alec. But the story of Alec's death grew in magnitude as we realized the depth of faith and service that resided in Alec's heart. He lived an austere and simple life so that he could help the poor and needy in China and Uganda. Even his parents didn't know the full extent of his charity and humble spirit until the letters poured in after his death. Many of us understand the Bible's calling to serve the poor and needy, but few will ever live it out in the fashion of a Mother Teresa. Alec had that passion. The good news – Dan and Izzie can move forward, proud of a son who lived a purposeful life.

Dr. Dan Johnson wrote the following tribute to his son Alec and I am privileged to share his story with you:

Alec Johnson, a 1993 graduate of Menomonie High School, who died on December 23rd, five days after his 40th birthday, was an astrophysicist working in fields so technically specialized that it was hard for his friends, even those with a science background, to grasp what he was up to. He had math going around in his head from grade school on through St. Olaf College and his graduation from

UW Madison with a PhD in Applied Mathematics in 2011. Math was Alec's gift and it could have been his ticket to a comfortable life at a prestigious university but along with his keen intelligence he held a radical belief in the Christian obligation to the poor. He took literally Jesus's statement, "What you do unto the least of these, you do unto me." And so Alec led a rather unusual life.

At UW Madison, while refining a program for solving nonlinear differential equations and creating mathematical models of the interaction of high-speed ions (bare atoms) moving fast through magnetic fields, he befriended the handicapped and the poor. He got interested in the plight of poor children in Haiti. He helped a colleague, Dr. Tonghai Yang, establish the Hometown Education Foundation, to support school children in rural China. For a year Alec lived as a homeless person in Madison in order to better understand their lives. He learned how to sleep on bare floors without blanket or mattress. He learned to live with the bare minimum of possessions.

A long-time friend of Alec's in Madison said, "Alec had the mind of Christ with a depth and obedience I've never seen. It was not something he 'put on' in situations. It permeated all his being, whether worshiping or at a baseball game. He showed me how to be a true friend to people we might think of as projects – lonely people to whom we might feel a duty."

His career led him to Belgium and the Catholic University of Leuven, where he did important groundwork useful in the design of nuclear-fusion containment vessels – one of humankind's hopes for clean energy – and also used to predict the effects of the material ejected from solar flares ("sunspots") on the earth's magnetic fields. Strong solar flares can damage satellites, computers, and the electrical power grid. Predicting whether they will hit the earth, and if so, when and how strongly, allows equipment to be shut down to decrease damage.

In Belgium, he worked with the DEEP-ER supercomputer project of the European Union to speed up programs running on "grids" made up of thousands of computers. At the same time, he developed ties to the poor of Uganda, made numerous trips there, and gave most of his income to provide scholarships to Ugandan students and to promote sustainable farming.

He traveled the world with only a tablet computer and a small backpack. He made friends whom he deeply cared for including Anywarach Joshua Carter with whom he collaborated on care for Ugandan orphans, and enjoyed long conversations about health, agriculture, community development, and education.

Out of his own pocket, Alec funded scholarships for about 60 students from grade school into college who could not have otherwise attended school. He paid for school gardens, tree nurseries, and donated the land for a coffee nursery that last year gave out 360,000 seedlings to the poor. He planned to buy land for a high school for the needy, with enough acreage to permit farming. His plan at his death was to teach university mathematics in Uganda.

Alec was willing to be taken advantage of – once. After that, he always had work that the person could do to earn more. "They reveal themselves," he said wryly. He began a goat project in Uganda, requiring that when the goat had a kid, it was to be given to another family to grow the project naturally.

In the DEEP-ER project, Alec was leading work on a really hard and important problem. "He was doing great work," said his supervisor, Dr. Giovanni Lapenta, "and we will be lost without him."

The day before Alec died, one of his Ugandan friends had a dream that Alec visited the St. Augustine community in Uganda and wished them farewell, saying he had now assigned someone else to take over. Anyone who wishes to help support his work can contact his mother at **isa@danlj.org**, or his father at **danlj@danlj.org**.

Alec's essays and extensive travelogues are available on his personal web page, http://www.danlj.org/eaj

A web page has been established to help continue Alec's project interests: **www.cultivating-community.org** – this has summaries and links.

***

Do you have family members who have developed values of charity, generosity, service to the poor and needy that inspires you and makes you proud that they are part of your family?

What are your experiences with sudden, tragic death of young people?

What are your experiences with a dream or premonition that foretold a future event? How do you think that happens?

32. The power of prayer

January 13, 2015

I can think of three times in my life when God seemed to answer prayer in a sudden and dramatic fashion. It clustered around three episodes of recurrent appendicitis that occurred during my time as a family medicine resident. The first episode developed one morning in Sioux Falls, SD. I awoke with no appetite and with a constant abdominal pain that quickly settled into my right lower abdomen. I went in to the family medicine clinic where I worked. My symptoms, physical exam and bloodwork all pointed to the diagnosis of acute appendicitis. I was told to drive to the hospital to be admitted for an appendectomy.

As Amy and I drove from the clinic to the hospital, I prayed for God to help me through my upcoming surgery. The pain immediately disappeared. I actually spent a pain-free night in the hospital because no one could believe that after three painful hours the appendicitis attack would spontaneously resolve. There was no surgery.

The next occurrence arose a couple of months later on the morning of my brother Dan's wedding. I was best man. The family left for the church for pictures, and I stayed back wondering at what point I should head over to the emergency room. The pain had been building up for two hours, so I prayed, and the pain dissipated. I made it to the church and spent the rest of the day enjoying the wedding celebration.

The third episode of appendicitis happened when I was on an obstetrics rotation in Houston, TX. I really didn't want to have my appendix taken out while alone in Houston. I waited one hour into the episode, prayed, and for a third time, the pain immediately resolved.

I eventually elected to have my appendix removed. We would be heading to Africa within months, and I didn't want surgery there. The pathology report confirmed that my appendix had been inflamed and infected.

Why did this happen? I ultimately ended up in the operating room having my appendix removed. It did take three episodes to completely convince me that the sudden dissolution of pain at the time of prayer wasn't just some odd coincidence. Prior to that time, I sometimes wondered if my prayers were traveling down the "bridge to nowhere." I needed something dramatic like this to convince me that God hears and answers our prayers.

Despite this dramatic evidence of the power of prayer, I remain undisciplined in my prayer life. Although I pray at church services or before larger meals (I can't give you a rational explanation why I almost never pray before eating breakfast), I don't have a consistent prayer time. I see a patient in the clinic who is suffering, and I pray a brief, silent prayer for God's help. God knows my heart and mind better than I, and I am convinced He doesn't need eloquence in my prayers. He also doesn't need me to tell Him what He needs to do to help. I also believe that He forgives my unfaithfulness in not leading a more robust prayer life. I relate well to Romans 8:26, "...FOR WE DO NOT KNOW HOW TO PRAY AS WE OUGHT, BUT THE SPIRIT HIMSELF INTERCEDES FOR US WITH SIGHS TOO DEEP FOR WORDS."

Most people would assume that I would be praying for a cure for my cancer, especially after believing that God had chosen three episodes of recurrent appendicitis to convince me of the power of prayer. With my first two episodes of appendicitis, I was praying for my recovery from surgery. When the pain of appendicitis suddenly resolved, I realized that God's answer to prayer was very different from the surgical response that I had anticipated with each episode of appendicitis. God's will and answer to our prayers is often different than our requests.

We are confused by the subject of prayer and healing. We read about many episodes of Jesus healing physical ailments in the New Testament. Jesus heals to show the power of God or to respond to someone's faith, or to elevate the afflicted and downtrodden. I fast forward today, and I wonder why people who are more saintly than I can pray fervently and still experience great suffering and sorrow in their lives. Yet I understand that they received comfort from God, spiritual renewal, and eventually a heavenly home where their pain and suffering vanished. It is these gifts from God that make prayer important in our lives.

Praying changes me by strengthening my faith in God and making prayer important in my life. I like to think that God appreciates my communication with Him through prayer. I know that when I pray, I am God's hands and feet on earth and shouldn't just sit back and wait for God to do something. I should be active in helping others whom I lift up in prayer.

I believe that God has been answering many prayers throughout my journey with cancer. I feel more blessed today than I did before having cancer. We should probably spend much more time thanking and praising God and less time asking for specific requests and favors from God. God understands our humanness. If we had faith as large as a grain of mustard seed, we could move mountains and nothing would be impossible (Matt. 17:20). It is a time in my life to acknowledge that I am not a particularly faithful person but fortunately live under the grace of God who forgives my shortcomings and hears my prayers. The answer to those prayers will be God's answer, not mine.

***

What is your prayer life like?

What experiences have you had when you were confident that God had intervened in a supernatural way in answering your prayer?

How does God answer prayer?

How do we truly know God's answers?

Did the people healed by Jesus eventually die? Why?

33. Monster

January 21, 2015

Amy and I are living in Mesa, Arizona for three weeks. Lounging isn't my forte. We are hiking and enjoying the outdoors of an Arizona January while appreciating that my previously wasted muscles continue to fill out and find new life.

The last 100- mile ultramarathon that I ran was the Javelina Jundred on October 27, 2012, in McDowell Mountain Regional Park near Phoenix, AZ. My friend Terry Sullivan and I ran together for the first 100 kilometers (62 miles) until a knee injury forced Terry to the sidelines. I continued on alone, running into the night.

As I have aged, my biggest issue in a 100- mile race is my sleepiness in the middle of the night. In the story of the tortoise and the hare, I would be the hare. I run, get sleepy, and then sit down at an aid station for naps that have lasted up to one hour. I have taken as many as three naps in the middle of the never-ending night that tests your mental will as much as your physical stamina.

During the night, I missed not having Terry's engaging chatter which would help to keep me awake. I had booked an early afternoon flight back to the Midwest the next day. If I slowed down too much, I risked missing my flight. Compounding the night's issues was the question that always hits at this difficult point in a race, "Why am I doing this?" Excuses were beginning to pile up for a final assault on my tired brain.

Help at a time like this can come in many forms. It might be as simple as some added calories in food and drink, encouraging conversation with another runner, support from an aid station volunteer, or sometimes a feeling from within. That feeling from within usually tells me that the emptiness felt tomorrow by choosing to not finish the race will be worse than any fatigue or discomfort that I'm experiencing at that point in the race.

I was more sleepy than usual that night. I was twenty minutes into my second nap of a night that was still young when I felt a tap on my chest. I awoke startled and saw an old running acquaintance, Pam Reed, staring at me. With disapproval in her voice, she said, "Dave, you aren't going to get to the finish line sleeping in this chair. Come run with me."

Pam Reed is a legend in the ultrarunning community. In 2006, I felt both humbled and honored when she asked me to be part of her crew at the Badwater 135- mile race run in the stifling heat of Death Valley and finishing on top of Mount Whitney. Considered one of the toughest endurance events in the country, Pam had won the race twice – beating everyone, including all the men.

In 2005, she became the first human on earth to run 300-miles continuously without sleep. When I ran alongside her crewing at Badwater, I asked her how she could possibly keep going for 78 straight hours without sleep and cover 300 miles. "Red Bull, lots of Red Bull," she replied without hesitation.

Pam and I began running together in the middle of that endless Arizona night. I was so sleepy that I could barely keep my eyes open. Pam told me to stay with her for ten miles until we got to an aid station where she had a surprise for me. We arrived together, and she reached into her duffle bag pulling out Red Bull's closest cousin, a Monster energy drink. "Here, drink this," she said.

I had never had an energy drink in my life but at 3AM and with twenty miles left in the race, there was no time like the present to introduce myself to Monster. The results were impressive. I was wide awake, super-charged, and had no difficulty finishing the 100- mile race. I am not advocating that you start pounding down energy drinks filled with sugar, caffeine and other "natural" stimulants. But I do know that the drudgery of a night that was demanding sleep was rescued by an energy drink.

I had a chance to thank Pam for her timely can of Monster. Without that opportunity, she would have never known that something that seemed so small and inconsequential had helped me so much. We often don't know how much our small acts of kindness or words of wisdom mean to those who receive it.

I am signed up to run another 100- mile race in Arizona, the Coldwater Rumble 100- miler on January 24. When two of my running friends, Terry Sullivan and Rolf Morck, found out that Amy and I were renting a house near the race, they decided to come down and test our mettle in another Arizona race. I have always considered these to be more of an event than a race. I will enjoy the company of two friends, take in the scenery of the dusty desert trail, and chat up some aid station volunteers. Unlike previous races, I have no idea how far I can go. If I thought that I had excuses before, I have now added a whole new list. This time, having benefited from another ultrarunner's experience, I will tuck a can of Monster into my duffle bag. And I will accept any other help or kindness that may come my way.

***

What do you think of people who run 100-miles for 'fun?'

What physical, spiritual, or mental challenges are there in your life, which inspire a sense of accomplishment?

What is the best advice a coach or another mentor has given to you?

34. Carpe Diem

January 28, 2015

Last Saturday, I ran the Coldwater Rumble 100- mile race through Estrella Mountain Regional Park in Goodyear, Arizona.

It seemed almost surreal to be back in another ultramarathon, running with friends, recounting previous adventures, and lightheartedly teasing each other. One year ago, I had no desire to ever run another ultramarathon again. The chemotherapy that I took in the fall of 2013 caused extreme fatigue and nausea. It felt so similar to what I have experienced in the middle of the night nearing the end of a 100 mile race, that I was sure that I would never do it again.

By the summer of 2014, I had lost so much muscle from cancer and its treatment that I quit running altogether. I still walked for exercise, but even running a couple miles felt weary and uncomfortable. I relinquished my lifetime entry to Grandma's Marathon and gave away my favorite running shoes to a friend. I had very little motivation to start running again.

It was in October that I stepped on the scale at one of my chemotherapy appointments. I had already noticed some thigh muscle starting to come back and was shocked to see that I had gained thirteen pounds since the summer. One month later, I ran the Rails to Trails Marathon, a memorable event, solidifying the fact that my running days weren't over.

When friends Rolf Morck and Terry Sullivan decided to come down to Arizona to run a 100- mile race, I knew that I wanted to enjoy the day running with them. There is an old African proverb that says, "If you want to go quickly, go alone. If you want to go far, go together." The Coldwater Rumble would be a journey together.

In 1999, I ran a 100- kilometer (62 mile) race from Florence to Faenza in Northern Italy. To my surprise, there were 3000 entrants, mostly Italians, making it a larger field than any ultramarathon in the US. I ran well that day but was equally surprised to find out that there were only 800 finishers. It was obvious that many Italians signed up knowing that they couldn't finish a race of that length. They registered anyway to take part in an event, not a race. When the starting gun went off, we ran into the streets of Florence. The roads weren't closed, but the traffic stopped as several thousand Italian runners poured through the streets, pumping their fists and yelling "Bravo." The race followed a mountain road through villages that held community bonfires in the night as entire families welcomed runners coming through their town. Peering into valleys on a moonlit night, I found the night portion of the race enchanting. The runners were there to relish this festive event and to see how far they could run. Getting to the 100- kilometer finish line wasn't the all-consuming goal for most of the runners.

Italians didn't have the same fear of failure that permeates our competitive American society. They lived to savor the day. Amy even observed one Italian runner who took a rest break during the race to smoke a cigar. At the finish line, I received three bottles of Italian wine. My bottles came home with me, but I suspect that many Italian runners consumed the wine with friends or family at the conclusion of the race to commemorate the achievement. The last two aid stations even served wine as a drink option in little plastic wine chalices. Why would an Italian wait until the end of the race to start celebrating?

The Coldwater Rumble 100- mile race was the first American race that I have run where fewer than 50% of the runners completed the race, even though a 100 mile trail race is much more difficult than the 100- kilometer road race that I ran in Italy. Unlike Italians, most Americans who sign up for ultramarathons expect to reach the finish line. They are driven to experience success.

Our fear of failure shields us from opportunities to succeed or from doing something epic. Surveys have shown that the greatest fear is public speaking, and it is ranked ahead of death. According to Jerry Seinfeld, "This means to the average person, if you go to a funeral, you're better off in the casket than doing the eulogy." We are afraid of being viewed as deficient or inadequate and cringe at the thought of feeling embarrassment or rejection. We hunker down into comfortable lives of routine that don't risk being embarrassed by the lack of success. We avoid the possibility of failure as if it were a plague.

Carpe diem – "seize the day" is an old Latin term which means that we should enjoy the pleasures of the moment without concern for the future. That definition was too Italian for American tastes. In the 1989 movie DEAD POETS SOCIETY, the English teacher John Keating, played by Robin Williams, says emphatically: "Carpe diem. Seize the day, boys. Make your lives extraordinary." American filmmaking took a very Italian "enjoy the day" and turned it into an American cry to do something epic today.

I signed up for the Coldwater Rumble 100-mile race with the attitude of an Italian. Carpe diem – seize the day. Yes, I wanted to do something epic, but if I fell short of 100 miles, the day would still be glorious. There was no shame in not finishing the race. It was an event to be savored, another adventure to be cherished, complete with the esprit de corps that accompanies a group of people encouraging each other onward. "Quit" is a dirty four-letter word in an American ultramarathon. Saturday, we may have quit before the finish line, but didn't fail. We stepped off the course at 60 miles, grateful for another great experience alongside friends. I didn't have to be Italian to treasure a "failed" attempt at 100 miles.

***

When has a fear of failure held you back from doing something?

Explain an event or day in which you lived out 'carpe diem.'

In what ways can 'success' be defined, even if to others, it may be viewed as 'failure.'

35. Ferris Bueller's Day Off

February 5, 2015

One of my favorite movies of all time is FERRIS BUELLER'S DAY OFF. Ferris fakes an illness to skip a day of high school and packs a day with so much fun and excitement that it would be the envy of any kid today. At the end of the movie, Ferris turns to the camera and says, "Life moves pretty fast. If you don't stop and look around once in a while, you could miss it." I love that line.

I don't suffer from seasonal affective disorder, but I do find that in the middle of winter, cabin fever hits pretty hard. It is a malaise up north where some people become less ambitious and long for spring. Since becoming a family physician in Menomonie twenty-eight years ago, I have never taken two consecutive weeks of vacation. Some years we have travelled south during the winter, but most years it hasn't happened.

Being afflicted with cancer isn't all bad. Amy and I just spent three weeks in Mesa, Arizona, and are now in Steamboat Springs, Colorado skiing. Many people who live with a disabling chronic illness find that their loss of productivity in life is troubling. I must admit that it was difficult for me to accept retirement after I was forced out of work with my cancer. To soothe any early retirement woes, I found there is nothing like spending three weeks in sunny Arizona in the midst of a cold Wisconsin winter.

Amy and I rented a house with my brother Dan and his wife Patricia. We went to Barrett-Jackson and Gooding classic auto auctions, watched an amateur golfer hit a hole-in-one on the famous 16th hole of the Phoenix Pro-Am tournament, and toured Frank Lloyd Wright's Taliesin West. We perused fine art at an open-air exhibit. I ran the Arizona Rock 'n' Roll half marathon that featured live rock bands throughout the course and joined two friends for a

60- mile running adventure in Estrella Mountain Regional Park. Some more friends came down, and we hiked numerous trails including scaling Camelback Mountain in Phoenix. We laughed, enjoyed each other's company, and basked in the warm, sunny weather.

When March and April rolled around, the snowbirds returned home to Wisconsin, and I would see them in the clinic. Most of them told me how much they were exercising down south. Their diabetes was better controlled, and they had shed a few pounds. There was something energizing about living down south in a beautiful climate and setting. I think I now understand.

This week Amy and I are skiing in Steamboat Springs, Colorado. Downhill skiing is my favorite sport, and our annual trip to Steamboat with our friends Mark Flaten and Lisa Novotny is always one of the best weeks of the year. Joining us this year are our sons Nathan and Eric and Eric's fiancée Sarah. We are delighted to have the time together with family and friends.

Skiing is just the right mix of adventurous physical exertion on the ski slopes and camaraderie on the chair lifts and in the chalet. At the end of the day, relaxing in the hot tub with a restorative beverage followed by supper establishes a rhythm that belies the perfect vacation.

Once each week in Colorado, Mark and I head out to ski a double black diamond run. I am not an expert skier and don't belong on an expert run. The challenge of denying our age and vulnerabilities sends us out on this annual adventure. We take off our skis after scooting off the chairlift and climb a steep path. Eventually we are at the highest point on the mountain and stare down at the precipitous slope below.

Two years ago, when we two old guys trekked to the top of the run, we came upon a group of young snowboarders in their baggy pants. They offered Mark and me some pot. We laughed and declined saying that we were scared to death to ski down the hill stone cold sober, much less while high. One of the snowboarders replied, "No, man, it just makes the trip better." We still passed on sharing a joint with the younger crowd. I was reminded of humorist Dave Barry saying, "Skiing combines outdoor fun with knocking down trees with your face." We didn't want to do anything that would make the trees harder to avoid.

I am struck this year by how much time Amy and I have spent with family. If cancer had not entered our lives, we would have missed out on many family times that I cherish and that our family will remember long after I am gone. Despite my dislike for the trials brought on by this illness and its treatment, our family time has been precious and would not have been possible without being gifted with the extra time chemotherapy has granted me.

These last three weeks are as close as I will ever get to living a Ferris Bueller's day off. I wish all of you could enjoy the same. "Life moves pretty fast. If you don't stop and look around once in a while, you could miss it."

***

What trip have you taken that was the most fun and adventurous?

What is on your bucket list?

36. Facing life's "interesting" challenges

February 16, 2015

At the end of head and neck radiation on October 1, 2013, I received a Certificate of Completion from the Mayo Clinic Department of Radiation Oncology. It read, "CHALLENGES ARE WHAT MAKE LIFE INTERESTING; OVERCOMING THEM IS WHAT MAKES LIFE MEANINGFUL." –Joshua J. Marine.

I was in the middle of the biggest challenge of my life, and I certainly wouldn't have chosen the word "interesting" to describe it. The pain was worsening daily. My mouth was morphing into a canker sore that eventually consumed my entire swollen tongue and cheeks. I had rapidly bumped up the dose of narcotic pain relievers to temper the severe mouth and throat pain. The narcotics just led to more vomiting and weight loss even with all of my nourishment being fed through a gastrostomy tube. I could only sleep at night when I took extra morphine but would awaken an hour later choking on the mucous exuding from the open sores in my mouth and throat. I talked to my oncologist, and we discussed whether I needed to be in the hospital. Did I find this challenge interesting? I certainly did not.

I surmised that Mr. Marine was referring to the lesser challenges of life that are self-imposed, not someone suffering from severe side effects at the completion of chemotherapy and head and neck radiation.

Many cancer patients have difficult challenges thrust upon them that are not of their own choosing. We start down a path of therapy, hoping and praying that we are the lucky ones. We will be the ones cured, the ones who suffer few side effects, or the ones to thrive and see our lives ingratiated with improved health and a longer life. For those who die from cancer, the reality of this progressive disease eventually overtakes the hope that cancer treatment will lead to a better life.

The difficulty in being confronted by suffering from cancer or a chronic illness is that we can't always overcome the challenges of the disease. Sometimes overcoming the challenge is really an acceptance of the condition. We learn to live with symptoms from our illness and its treatment. We understand that our lives can't be driven by productivity and that we may become more dependent on others. We make peace with reality.

Having observed the struggles of many patients, I am reminded that there is always someone whose cross to bear is greater than mine. Yet I have also been impressed with how some people, despite the overbearing weight of their cross, are still able to live their lives more fully than others. We are not passively waiting to die. We must rise above the illness in our bodies. It requires perseverance with hope fueling an internal drive to move us beyond surviving to thriving. We can accept our condition and thrive in life at the same time. God's energy flows through us to live in the richness of each day and to look forward to another tomorrow.

We make a daily choice of how we live our lives. When we live in the moment, we can choose not to fret or to dwell on an uncertain future. We should be passionate about our lives and what we do. When we are passionate, we make sacrifices so we can lead meaningful and joyous lives.

In life, I have always savored the opportunity to prepare for the next challenge. I am thrilled by achieving the things I could not be sure were possible. I like going beyond what I have already mastered, seeking out new horizons. These are self-imposed challenges. They are different from the challenges imposed by my cancer and its treatment. They are different from many of life's trials that are thrust in our direction: experiencing the loss of jobs or relationships, grieving the death of loved ones, or living with chronic pain or illness.

Some adults grow comfortable in life and quit searching out new challenges and quit preparing for new opportunities. If we live without goals or have no willingness to undertake the challenges necessary to meet those goals, then we end up bored with our subdued lives. I suspect that this is the reason that I still want to run an ultramarathon or ski double black diamond ski runs. I want Amy to have a smooth transition in life when I am finally laid to rest. That goal led me to spend days in our yard last fall cutting out buckthorn, spreading new mulch, storing up firewood and adding onto our woodshed. The challenge was soldiering on to complete those tasks, despite feeling fatigued from cancer and chemotherapy.

To this end, I can look at the quote from Joshua J. Marine and it makes sense: "CHALLENGES ARE WHAT MAKE LIFE INTERESTING; OVERCOMING THEM IS WHAT MAKES LIFE MEANINGFUL." I wouldn't give out a certificate with this particular quote to someone suffering greatly from radiation therapy, but I would give it to someone who isn't seeking out new self-imposed challenges in their lives.

***

Aging can lead to dependence on others. How willing will you be to accept help from others?

What self-imposed challenges are there in your life?

In what ways do you live in the moment? Worry about the future? Re-live the past with regrets?

37. Hope reigns

February 24, 2015

In the book DEATH FORETOLD: PROPHECY AND PROGNOSIS IN MEDICAL CARE, sociologist and physician Nicholas Christakis queried the physicians of almost 500 terminally ill patients to determine how long they thought their patient would survive. When Dr. Christakis followed up on those patients, he found that only 17% of the physicians underestimated their patient's survival time; 63% overestimated it. The average estimate was 530% too high. In another study, oncologists overestimated survival by six months. These overly optimistic prognoses may adversely affect patient decision-making and the quality of care near the end of life.

A prediction of time left in life for a terminally ill patient is merely an average on what is typically a very broad bell-shaped curve. My oncologist, Dr. Sandeep Basu, has given me very accurate expectations according to the medical literature. After starting my current chemotherapy regimen in May 2014, he estimated that I had 9-12 months to live. When I fact-checked the prognosis statistics for similar patients on my kind of chemotherapy, they lived an average of ten months. I appreciate not just his honesty but the fact that he has done his homework.

Why are doctors often overly optimistic in their prognosis to terminally ill patients? We want to give patients hope. We don't want to let patients down. We prefer not to confront the mortality of our patient, which involves long conversation and perhaps an air of pessimism about their future. The future is still unknown. Although the average patient who is terminally ill may not live long, there are always some outliers who are going to live well beyond the average prognosis. In rare cases, cancers are cured when it was entirely unexpected.

Sometimes physicians feel like they are in a competition with other healthcare providers. We aren't the only game in town. When we give a patient little hope for an extended life, they may seek other opinions. There are many entrepreneurial practitioners worldwide who will give hope, promise cures, and boast that there are no side effects to their natural treatments. The internet is full of cures for incurable cancer. There are herbs, pills, vitamins, enzymes, vaccines, teas, high colonics, hyperthermia, meditation, restrictive diets, and a multitude of technologic machines with scientific-sounding names. These treatments purport to detoxify, to bolster immune systems, and to turn cancer cells into healthy cells. Although there are alternative and complementary medicine practices that have helped many cancer patients improve the quality of their lives, we should all be wary of charlatans who tout cancer cures.

Modern medicine does not dispute that there are many health habits that are good for cancer patients. A well-balanced diet, moderate exercise, adequate sleep, less stress and a positive attitude in life are healthy behaviors and should be practiced by those who are sick and those who are well. Unfortunately, because many medical cancer treatments are harsh, it is easy to understand that there is a huge draw to believe that terminal cancer will be cured by treatments that promise hope and that deny the downside of side effects.

Many Americans are distrustful of the scientific method. We are sometimes whipsawed by the results of scientific inquiries and studies. The latest dietary guidelines now say that moderate coffee consumption is good and that the cholesterol in egg yolks isn't as bad as we had previously believed. Tens of thousands of chemicals have been tested as possible chemotherapies but very few end up showing promise. Pharmaceutical companies report that bringing a new chemotherapeutic drug to market costs over one billion dollars. Multiple preclinical and clinical trials must be passed to show that the efficacy of the drug outweighs its side effects before the FDA will approve it. Yet, with all of this science supporting a chemotherapeutic drug, cancer patients can turn to completely untested theories on the internet and cling to them. They offer hope and testimonials without any scientific rigor that would come even remotely close to FDA approval. The scientific world still has much to understand about cancer, but we shouldn't abandon the scientific method in determining what treatment works and what doesn't.

Where does that leave prayer? The scientific method has been used to study prayer. Studies have shown that cancer patients who pray or who are supported in prayer report a better quality of life and less depression. When patients live longer than expected, we like to believe that it was God's answer to our prayers. Unfortunately, it leaves us demoralized when a faithful person dies more quickly than expected. When God doesn't answer those prayers in the way that we would like, we may become frustrated or disillusioned. When we are disappointed that God has not granted us concessions in life, we belittle God.

God has greater plans for us. I suspect that there is much more spiritual than physical healing in us as the result of prayer. When we pray zealously to be cured, we are actually praying that we can stay on earth and avoid, for a time, God's promise of heaven. I wonder what God thinks about that.

***

If you had only a few months to live, what plans would you make?

If facing a serious illness, would you seek alternative treatments outside of the U.S.? Why or why not?

How do you understand God's promise of a much better life in heaven after death?

38. Free clinic

March 3, 2015

Last weekend, the Free Clinic of the Greater Menomonie Area celebrated the tenth anniversary with its annual benefit auction. I remember my first day working at the free clinic ten years ago. My second patient seen that day was a young woman. We barely got through introductions before she asked me, "How much will this cost?" I told her that the visit, lab work and medications were all free. She started to cry. Through her tears she asked, "Are you sure?"

I excused myself from the room to talk to our head nurse. It was the first month of operation, and I was new to the clinic. I wanted to make sure that I had spoken correctly. "Yes," she said, "it is all free." I stepped back into the exam room and told her that all of her care was covered by the free clinic. There would be no bills. Once again, she started to cry.

When I first started seeing patients at the free clinic, I may have presumed that I would be seeing a lot of people who were struggling in life because of low intellect, mental illness, drug and alcohol issues, or lack of motivation. This was the first of many patients who would shatter anyone's stereotype of a free clinic patient. She was smart, articulate and driven. She previously held an excellent well-paying job bolstered by generous medical insurance. Then she developed chronic health problems. When her health deteriorated, she lost her job but still strove to be productive. She settled for a low-paying job without benefits. The medical bills escalated. Bill collectors harassed her regularly, trying to pull her last dollars out of her pocket. Her body was failing her, but her fighting spirit and will to work were relentless.

If there ever had been any question as to how often I would volunteer at the free clinic, this young lady had put that question to rest. From that day forward, I vowed to work as often as I was needed.

I have a newfound respect for the crushing power of medical bills. The medical bills for the first six months of my tongue cancer treatment totaled about a quarter of a million dollars. I underwent major surgery, hospitalization, gastrostomy tube placement, chemotherapy and thirty radiation treatments. I am not as expensive as I used to be. I now have chemotherapy every three weeks at a cost of merely $6000 per treatment. I am grateful for all of these treatments, and likely wouldn't be here today without the continued chemotherapy. Thank goodness, I have very good health insurance through the Mayo Clinic. Without health insurance, most families couldn't pay for the cost of my cancer care. Too many families are one major illness away from financial collapse.

At least half of all US bankruptcies are because of health problems and medical bills. The Affordable Care Act (Obamacare) may make a dent in this statistic, but many people are still underinsured. Already we have seen a significant drop in the number of people using the free clinic because of the ACA, but the need for care in the free clinic is not going away.

One of the medical students who worked with me commented that their medical school class had an interesting debate in a medical ethics course. The question before them was, "Should healthcare in the United States be a right or a privilege?" Should healthcare be a right of all citizens or just a privilege to those who can afford it? I was saddened to hear that there wasn't more altruism in the handful of young medical students who believed that healthcare should be a privilege. The pragmatic argument used by the medical students who supported healthcare as a privilege asked the pointed question, "Who will run a healthcare system that delivers affordable healthcare to everyone?" Do you trust greedy insurance companies or do you trust a dysfunctional federal government?

Pick your poison: insurance companies or government or both. Innocent people who lose their health shouldn't have their agony compounded by impoverishing their families. The Affordable Care Act is making a difference in the lives of those who previously were uninsured but we are still a nation of privilege. It is time for Americans to stand behind universal health coverage and join the vast majority of the developed world. I hope I can live to see the day when the free clinics of this country can close their doors. In the meantime, I am back volunteering at the free clinic remembering the tears of joy and relief in a young lady I saw ten years ago.

One additional note: Bob Dahlke, a friend and master wood carver, gifted an eagle for the free clinic auction. Colleagues from Mayo Clinic – Red Cedar donated over $4000 to the free clinic to buy it and donate it to me. The generosity of Bob and my colleagues is humbling and appreciated. Thank you.

***

Are you aware of a person/family in a dire economic situation because of a catastrophic illness or injury?

Should healthcare in the U.S. be a right of all citizens, or remain a privilege to those who can afford it?

Is the Affordable Care Act (Obamacare) a step in the right, or wrong, direction?

39. Early retirement

March 11, 2015

I have subscribed to *Money* magazine for many years. I like the advice on how we should save and invest money. I like even more the message that we should be frugal in our spending habits. I especially appreciate the rare story of charitable giving that will occasionally flash across its pages. It does my heart good to see that a financial publication gives print space to charitable deeds and contributions. What I don't like is the overt presumption that everyone wants to retire early. In *Money* magazine, the goal of early retirement seems to be the primary motivator for growing your wealth.

As a family physician, it is true that your patients grow older with you. At my current age of fifty-seven, I saw many patients who were longing for retirement. In many cases, this yearning to retire was because of issues that surround a lifetime of work. Those doing physical labor were often feeling the aches and pains of a body that had broken down from years of use and abuse. Those who struggle under domineering bosses or in unfulfilling careers were also anxious to leave their jobs behind. Most often, it seemed like growing older was zapping the energy that in their youth had previously propelled them through long workdays.

One of the gratifying aspects of my medical career was that I never reached a time when I longed to retire. Although there were many long days, I didn't find myself looking at my watch, wondering when my workday would be done. Amy and I didn't talk about retirement or where we might live after I left my practice. At age 57, it wasn't on our radar.

Only in recent years did I begin to appreciate that this desire to continue working late into life is unusual in

American society. I can look back now and realize that it was the enduring relationships with patients, the conversations, the shared experiences, and the opportunity to help others that gave meaning to my work. I wish that everyone could be employed in a job that gives their lives this same level of purpose and connection to others.

I have known many people who reached retirement and then returned to work. The professor who continued writing books after leaving the classroom, the pressman who came back to work as a grocery stock boy and enjoyed working alongside kids who were fifty years younger, and the pastor who served as an interim pastor at several dozen congregations for twenty years after "retirement." The pastor's son told me that his father passed out once or twice in the pulpit in his 80s. He didn't quit. Instead he preached sitting down until the last year of his life when cancer forced him to stop.

Many retirees don't return to work that earns a paycheck but instead are the volunteers who create a tremendous amount of good in their communities. Feeling sidelined by cancer, I have a newfound respect for those who contribute their time, skills, and energy till late into life. They do so even when their weakened bodies dwindle to a shadow of their former self. They remain the hands and feet of many charitable organizations.

I recently received official word from my employer that I am not retired but am a disabled employee. I never requested retirement. My work as a family physician came to a halt this past May when my Mayo Clinic oncologist informed me that my cancer was now terminal and that I would never return to work. It wasn't a good day to be me. I was feeling physical pain, was handed a death sentence, and was told that I would never return to productive employment. Only the most Pollyannaish cancer patient could find a silver lining in her pronouncement that day.

I met with my local oncologist last week, and the news this time around was more hopeful. The results of my chemotherapy have been beyond anyone's expectations. The plan is to have a PET scan to look for any evidence of cancer in May. That will be one year since I started palliative chemotherapy. If I am that rare person with advanced recurrent head and neck cancer who goes into remission and has no evidence of cancer on that PET scan, it still will not mean that the cancer is cured. It would mean, however, that there is potentially a much longer time left in life. In the cancer world, it would be my entry point into unchartered territory.

I became gainfully unemployed when I was disabled by my cancer and its treatment. I didn't choose to retire but was too ill to work. Yet, in illness or in health, we all need to answer the question, "What am I going to do with the rest of my life?" I would like to answer that question, knowing that my cancer is in remission. Until then, I will continue to live life with cancer, one day at a time and to enjoy my "early retirement."

∗∗∗

What is the appeal of early retirement to some? To you?

What will give your life meaning and fulfillment in retirement?

40. Surrounded by kindness

March 19, 2015

Since being diagnosed with cancer, Amy and I have been overwhelmed by acts of kindness from others. I had chemotherapy last Friday, and my clinic nurses Barb Biesterveld and Jackie Weber stopped by over lunch hour. They have visited regularly since I started chemotherapy, even in the midst of their busy days. Barb brought in my mail from the clinic that included a gift from an anonymous donor. The card read, "Someone you know has contacted us anonymously at **Phil's Friends** to send you this gift of sunshine!" Phil's Friends offers prayers and a gift box filled with many items that cancer patients might need. Like the supportive prayers that our family receives, Amy and I may never know who sent the gift, but it is appreciated. Thank you.

Over a couple months last summer, friends Rob and Amy Mondlock set up a schedule at our church which members could bring flowers and a note to our door each day. We tried to catch the gift bearer at the door, but too often they left without an opportunity for us to chat or say thank you. The fragrant aroma of fresh flowers wafted through our house, and the personal notes were precious. Amy and I have received hundreds of cards and letters from friends, colleagues and extended family. These are among the most precious gifts that we have received.

I can't walk through our house without seeing reminders of the thoughtfulness of others. It is humbling to receive these selfless gifts. My two Texan nieces painted a landscape watercolor with the caption, "THE LORD IS MY REFUGE AND STRENGTH." – Psalm 46:1. It hangs over my dresser. My father has gifted numerous handmade treasures that grace our house. He built a wooden cremation urn out of red cedar and a matching wood frame to hold a picture of me. They were constructed in anticipation of my upcoming funeral. He cut down red cedar trees and took them to be milled and kiln dried. The lumber was consumed by fire when the kiln burned to the ground that night. He made another long trip to do it all over again before he could bring the red cedar into his woodshop to produce the finished products. It was truly a labor of love. My clinic contributed the personal photo that will go into the frame, and Kado Gallery donated the matting for the picture. Both refused any payment with the knowledge that I was terminally ill with cancer.

The goodwill of others is displayed by much more than gifts. Conversations with friends and family lift my spirits. There is joy in simply spending time with people. My journey with cancer has provided living proof that the kindness of others is alive and well in both words and deeds.

Like many of you, I have lived an adult life marked by independence without the need to be the recipient of charity. Although I appreciate the goodwill, it is difficult to accept so much generosity from others. It has become easier as I have grown to realize the great value of kindness in our lives. People around me have recognized that I am a human in need. They want to help. They see the opportunity to show compassion and to make a difference in my life. Research suggests that the person who shows kindness is rewarded as much as the person who is the recipient of their kindness. And yes, people do pay it forward, creating a more caring society. Our society stands on the backs of empathetic and compassionate people. These are the people who show hospitality to strangers, who care for those who are less fortunate, and who see the plight of the poor, the sick, the abandoned and the disenfranchised as a cause worthy of their time and effort. I am blessed to have many of these people in my life.

When we treat others with kindness and with no thought of reward, we change as humans. We live lives that have greater meaning and happiness. I am honored and humbled to be surrounded by family, friends, and an entire community that has shown Amy and me compassion and kindness in so many ways.

"KINDNESS IS THE LANGUAGE THAT THE DEAF CAN HEAR AND THE BLIND CAN SEE."

-MARK TWAIN

***

Tell of a time when you were on the receiving end of an act of kindness.

In what ways do you show kindness to others?

Why is it sometimes hard to accept acts of kindness from others?

Why is it important for each person to feel loved?

41. An uncertain life

March 26, 2015

There are many uncertainties in the cancer world. It begins with our current medical knowledge of cancer and its treatments. Scientists have identified specific genetic mutations that lead to various cancers but still have not been able to use that information to find a cure. Oncologists prescribe aggressive medical therapies to treat cancer, but they still can't predict which patient will benefit from the treatment and which will be doomed by cancer that continues to grow unchecked. We don't know who will breeze through treatment without much difficulty and who will experience life-threatening side effects. We still can't explain why people develop cancer. Genetics, environmental factors, and other risk factors don't provide more than a clue as to its true underlying cause.

When you develop cancer, the uncertainties surrounding cancer become personal. Why did I get cancer? Did I do something wrong? Will my cancer treatment work? If not, will there be another treatment? If I'm in remission, will the cancer return? Will the side effects that I am experiencing from cancer treatment be permanent? Will pain forever be a part of my life? How do I talk to others about my cancer? Is it too much of a downer to discuss it at all? Will I ever return to work or to a productive life? Will the cost of my medical care impoverish my family? Will the relationship with my spouse, family and friends change? Will I be a burden to others at the end of life? Will the struggle at life's end be more than I can withstand?

It is easy for me to understand why cancer patients attend support groups, seek counseling and pray.

Cancer or any serious illness is a reminder of the unpredictability of everything. I have worked in the ER, many times witnessing how quickly our lives can change direction. Accidents and illness can suddenly usher in a new reality. Our bodies are not permanent structures, and may break down, eventually giving out altogether. It is easy to bemoan the loss of health. Letting go of our expectations of vigor and productivity in our previous healthy life is a necessary step in living with a disabling illness or injury. The stumbling block of remembering our healthy past must be replaced by the stepping stones to our uncertain future.

Much of our angst from a chronic illness stems from our desire to resolve or at least improve our current condition. Some things in life can't be fixed. Sometimes the fix is a change in our attitude. Without a level of acceptance in our current condition, we can't move on to enjoy life in spite of illness.

My life with cancer is filled with uncertainty. Last summer, Amy and I never planned anything more than six weeks in advance. The likelihood of my cancer returning and altering our plans was too great. The longer that we have lived with an unpredictable future, the bolder we have become. I just signed up to attend an ultramarathon running camp in July. Will my cancer be back by July? I don't know. Will I be strong enough to participate? I don't know. I do know that I am not going to put my life on hold by anticipating the worst. I am still well enough to cherish life. I will make future plans based on unsure assumptions. We all live lives cloaked in uncertainty. Living with cancer just accentuates the uncertainty.

One year ago, left with a poor prognosis, chronic pain, and the grim anticipation of a horrible death, it would have been easy to focus on a pessimistic view of my future. Being anxious or depressed about a clouded future could have stolen months of life. Worrying does not free us from tomorrow's troubles, but it does rob us of today's peace. No matter how unclear our future becomes, we are challenged to live in the present, count our blessings and appreciate the joys of life. When we stop worrying about what can go wrong, we can become enthusiastic about what might go right. That's an attitude of uncertainty that we all can live with.

"DON'T WAIT. THE TIME WILL NEVER BE JUST RIGHT."

-Napoleon Hill

***

What do you worry about?

Do you tend to worry about other people, even if you are not in a position to change their predicament?

What is a good approach to dealing with uncertainty and anxiety?

42. In search of a better death

April 2, 2015

At the end of their lives, many patients receive aggressive medical treatments in an attempt to extend their lives. An American living with cancer has a 1in 4 chance of dying in a hospital and a similar chance of spending part of his last month in an intensive care unit. The chances are much higher if you suffer from chronic heart or lung disease.

Modern medicine has available a cache of weapons that can be pulled out of the arsenal and onto the battlefield up to the very last days of life. If your kidneys fail, we have dialysis. When your lungs fail, we have ventilators. When your heart is faltering, there are a myriad of drugs and possible surgeries, not to mention installing electronic devices like pacemakers and implantable defibrillators. If you can't swallow, there are feeding tubes. For cancer patients, there flows an endless stream of possible chemotherapies, some FDA approved and some still in investigational studies. And let's not forget radiation treatments and surgery. Although physicians fear being accused of doing too little, there is not enough acknowledgement that doing too much has the potential to be far more harmful to a dying patient.

Immortality will never be an attainable goal of treatment. Yet sometimes it is easier for physicians to give the patient and his family some degree of hope with an intensive treatment plan than to explain why allowing natural death with an emphasis on comfort would be the most prudent option. One thing is clear. Too many patients die suffering with pain and other symptoms that weren't adequately controlled. Tragically, there are also times when no one knew the true wishes of the patient, and overly aggressive forms of treatment were continued, even when death was imminent.

Some patients, however, do want very aggressive treatment to the end of life. Part of my journey as a physician was to learn not to judge others' choices. Some patients refuse to quit aggressive treatments because they are afraid of death. Some patients are in denial up until death but still do well psychologically by believing that they will continue to live. Some patients want to show their family how much they love them by refusing to "give up." A patient at the end of life may find great meaning in pushing herself hard; to celebrate that she is tougher than she ever felt was possible. Stuart Scott, the sportscaster who recently passed away at a young age, pointed out that many good fighters die from cancer. "When you die, it does not mean that you lose to cancer. You beat cancer by how you live, why you live and in the manner in which you live." Mahatma Gandhi said, "My life is my message." Sometimes I believe that a fight to the end is a patient's message that as long as I have life in my body, I will endure and persevere.

I find it helpful to remember that what we hope for changes naturally as we grow older. For many people, at first it was to be done with school, then to launch a career, to choose a mate, to have and to raise children, and see them spread their wings. With cancer or other terminal illnesses, we hope for a cure at first, then hope for lots of high quality time, then comfort.

The biggest upheaval in my thinking came with the realization that often late in an illness, more is less. There have been some remarkable studies that suggest that hospice and palliative care actually extend life. A 2010 study of 151 end-stage (stage 4) lung cancer patients showed that those randomized to receive palliative care lived 2.7 months longer. They also felt better and suffered less depression. A 2007 review of 4,493 Medicare patients found that those in hospice lived longer. Those with pancreatic cancer lived 3 weeks longer, lung cancer 6 weeks longer and congestive heart failure 3 months longer. Physicians should no longer discuss end-of-life options with the old "You could live longer or you could be comfortable" shtick. It may be more appropriate to advise folks that we really don't know for sure, but it may be that more technology may actually shorten one's life span.

High tech end-of life care isn't just expensive; it isn't meeting the full needs of patients and their families. Physicians tend to focus on physical aspects of care, but terminally ill patients tend to look at the end of life with broader spiritual and psychosocial meaning. Patients' primary goals at the end of life include being comfortable, strengthening relationships with family and friends, not being a burden to others, achieving a sense that life is complete, and making peace with God. Longevity isn't on their list of priorities. Dying in an ICU can be a full measure of failure when these primary goals are largely ignored in an effort to merely prolong a dying patient's life. It is time to build a medical system that more fully supports a comfortable and meaningful end-of-life, buttressed by the principles of hospice and palliative care.

***

Have you known of someone who died whose medical treatment seemed overly aggressive at the end of their life?

What was the goal of that treatment?

What is your idea of a 'good death'?

What are your goals at the end of life?

Do you think you'd choose to be made comfortable, or continue aggressive medical treatment, if there is still hope?

43. The road to hospice

April 9, 2015

During my early years as a family physician, I had a couple of contentious family conferences that involved a dying patient and his family. The typical scenario was a son who flew in from southern California and was astounded to see his father in such bad shape. Family members who lived locally and had provided care and support during their dad's gradual decline weren't shocked. When we discussed the goal of keeping dad comfortable, most of the family agreed. But the son couldn't understand why we couldn't "do more." I could tell that he felt guilty that he hadn't been more involved with his dad in the last months and years of his life. I had a sense that he now wanted to make it up to dad by insisting on more aggressive treatment. He seemed somewhat dismayed that a young family physician like me in a small Podunk Wisconsin town wasn't recommending transferring his father to a regional medical center to attempt life-extending treatment. He was sure that his dad would have received higher tech treatment at UCLA Medical Center. He probably was right.

I grew to realize that it was important for me to know the wishes of the dying patient. I determined that a patient was more likely to embrace death when three criteria were met:

1)   The inevitability of death: The patient had experienced a decline in health and knew that death was inevitable.

2)   Comfort was important: The patient had experienced suffering which often was physical such as pain but could also be psychological. We offered a plan to make the end of life more comfortable.

3)   Belief in heaven or an afterlife: I was impressed by how many elderly patients had a deep faith in God and

were confident of a life in heaven. It was reassuring to the family to hear that their loved one believed in heaven and wasn't fearful of the next step in his journey. Their loved one was ready to die.

I found that these three points of conversation created a trifecta that embraced death. If I entered a family conference with these three points clearly spelled out, families were more accepting that their loved one was drawing near to the end of life and that we could work together toward a more comfortable passing that maximized the limited time left with family.

According to surveys of terminally ill cancer patients, they prefer to die comfortably at home surrounded by people who love them. They don't want to be hooked up to uncomfortable tubes, awakened repetitively for vital signs, meds and tube checks in an ICU with limited visiting hours that create a loneliness unbecoming of a person dying. Unless physicians are told otherwise, the default plan is to push onward and continue aggressive treatment with the hope that it may prolong life. If medical personnel and families don't have the conversation to apply the brakes, this is the track that the train usually takes. This track, to fight to the bitter end, is so common that 36% of all patients admitted to hospice die within one week.

Too many people interpret the move to hospice care as giving up on life. Instead it should be viewed as a change in goals that is very appropriate when death looms on the horizon. Hospice teams specialize in alleviating symptoms such as pain and seeking to improve the quality of life for the terminally ill. Interestingly, studies suggest that patients in hospice care aren't just more comfortable, but also tend to live longer than those choosing aggressive treatments up until the time of death. Hospice care comes to the patient, usually at home, but also in a hospice unit, a nursing home or a hospital if needed to relieve suffering. Hospice embraces a holistic approach to care that involves a diverse team of professionals and volunteers. Grief and bereavement counseling is offered to families for thirteen months after the death of a loved one. It takes great courage and support for patients and their families to find peace in the midst of adversity. Hospice helps pave that road through death and beyond.

A study of people with advanced cancer in the US found that those who discussed end-of-life preferences with their physicians initiated a cascade of positive events. These initial conversations led to earlier hospice referral and less aggressive treatment at the end of life. These patients went on to report a better quality of life. Their caregivers also reported a better quality of life with less depression and regret six months after the death of their loved one. What began as a significant end-of-life discussion and earlier hospice referral helped bereaved caregivers live with less anguish months down the road.

Hospice care still has some drawbacks in the cancer world. Treatments given with potentially curative intent are not allowable under the Medicare Hospice Benefit, the primary payer for hospice care in the United States. There are now many more investigational treatments and trials of chemotherapy and immunotherapy that may offer hope, and fewer side effects and that may be appropriate for a cancer patient nearing the end of life. It is disappointing that outdated guidelines can force a patient to decide between another possible round of chemotherapy or hospice care.

As a physician, my professional experience with hospice has been very favorable. Given the difficult circumstances that surround death, I am impressed by the level of praise given to hospice by most families. The road to hospice, however, requires those initial conversations between patient, family, and health professionals. We shouldn't be shy about starting those conversations.

***

What have been your experiences with hospice?

Have there been situations in your family where there was disagreement over medical care at the end-of-life? How was is resolved?

How do you feel about you or a loved one dying at home?

How comfortable would you be with caregivers coming into your home (hospice) near the end of life?

44. "The needs of the patient come first"

April 16, 2015

As a physician, what is it like to now be the patient? My experience as a cancer patient began with surgery to remove my tongue cancer and neck lymph nodes on July 23, 2013, at a Mayo Clinic Hospital in Rochester, MN. I am grateful for its proximity to Menomonie; a short two hour drive. The Mayo Clinic may be the most recognized hospital system in the world and is a pillar of education, research and medical care. You don't have to be there for long to realize that people, having chosen Mayo for their medical care, come from all over the world. But lying on a hospital gurney before and after surgery had the feel of being on an assembly line. With 1265 beds and 55 operating rooms, how important could I be at Mayo's St. Mary's Hospital? Could a healthcare system this large offer personalized patient-centered care?

When the head and neck surgeon at the Mayo Clinic saw me, he recommended surgery. Since I was dealing with significant tongue pain, I requested it be done soon. Although the surgery was not an emergency, and would take four hours, and was a last minute add-on to the schedule, the surgery staff would accommodate our request. Surgery was scheduled for the next day. Amy and I were grateful. Patient 1 – Hospital Rules 0.

After surgery, I was thankful that my post-operative pain was manageable. I could finally stay asleep. I reviewed with my hospital nurse the schedule of multiple awakenings for that first night. I told my nurse that I was exhausted from lack of sleep. We agreed that when I woke at night, I would press the nurse call light and she would come in then to do her work. She would let me sleep until I awoke and contacted her. I was rested the next morning and felt much better. Patient 2 – Hospital Rules 0.

I was surprised to find out that simply taking a walk after my surgery relieved my post-operative pain. Instead of taking a pain pill, I went for eight walks that day with Amy. After roaming the hospital hallways for half a day, we asked the nursing staff if they would bend the rules and allow us to leave the hospital and walk the surrounding streets. They agreed, and we were able to enjoy the beautiful summer weather and local garden. They told me to leave my cell phone number on my hospital room door in case they needed to contact me. Instead of side effects from narcotic pain relievers, Amy and I were given permission to walk outside for pain control. Patient 3 – Hospital Rules 0.

The Mayo Clinic's core value is "The needs of the patient come first." I was impressed by the entire medical staff caring for me, endorsing a culture of patient-centered care and working to accommodate my unconventional requests. My safety wasn't compromised. It felt good to be a patient where a hospital rule wasn't used to squelch my needs.

I also experienced firsthand the importance of good physician and patient communication. I was seen by twenty physicians, medical residents and nurse practitioners during my first six months of cancer treatment. I had only one bad experience. I saw a general surgeon who was very paternalistic in his communication style. He wanted to place a gastrostomy feeding tube prior to starting my radiation and chemotherapy. Although it was likely that a feeding tube would be needed, he berated my hesitation to have it placed before knowing that I would need it. He was unable or unwilling to answer Amy's question: "How many of these feeding tubes are actually used?" and made her feel stupid for even asking the question. He also made dismissive comments about my Mayo Clinic radiation oncologist who had recommended having it placed later. It was his way or the highway. Amy and I chose the highway.

Instead we saw his partner who engaged us in shared decision-making. We reviewed the pros and cons of placing a gastrostomy tube now or later. We ended up having it placed several weeks later at a time when it became clear that I would need it. Amy and I were confident it was a good decision after having the kind of open and informative discussion that all patients should expect from their doctor.

My experience as a physician/patient is a reminder to all patients that it is OK to speak up for yourself and to advocate for your own healthcare. Patients should feel free to verbalize their questions and concerns. Your medical care should feel like it is a partnership between healthcare workers and yourself. Collaborative care makes for better care.

Mayo's core value, "The needs of the patient come first," was first articulated as the guiding principle of the Mayo practice in 1910 by Dr. William J. Mayo. Its longevity of over 100 years tells us that it is more than just another customer service slogan. It is the foundation of a culture that reminds all of us in healthcare that we are privileged to work for the patients we serve. It fosters an environment of caring, collaboration, excellence, and continuous improvement. I have been blessed to live under this core value as both a family physician and as a patient.

"THE BEST INTEREST OF THE PATIENT IS THE ONLY INTEREST TO BE CONSIDERED, AND IN ORDER THAT THE SICK MAY HAVE THE BENEFIT OF ADVANCING KNOWLEDGE, UNION OF FORCES IS NECESSARY."

-William J. Mayo, MD,

Rush Medical College Commencement, 1910

***

How well does your healthcare provider act as if "the needs of the patient come first?"

How easy is it for you to speak up, ask questions, and advocate for yourself?

What experiences have you where you wished you had spoken up?

45. Chemo week: Two steps forward, one step back

April 23, 2015

When Amy and I lived in Cameroon Africa, we participated in Sunday morning church services that lasted several hours. It always began with the choir processing into the church. They started blocks away and, as they sang, would march two steps forward and one step back. It could take them up to forty-five minutes to enter the church and sit down. I have only so much patience. In typical American fashion, I would look at them and think, "Could you pick up the pace? We don't have all day. I have places to go, things to do and people to see." During the worship service, if the pastor didn't see enough money in the offering plate, the plate was passed around again, and again, and again. All was not lost. We returned to the United States thankful for one-hour worship services and appreciative that the offering plate is passed around only once.

My chemotherapy is like the Cameroon choir processional. Instead of two steps forward and one step back, it is two weeks forward and one week back. I receive chemotherapy every three weeks. The first week after chemo is typical of many cancer patients who are putting a poison into their body. Amy and I call this week "chemo week." Fortunately, my one week backward is followed by two weeks forward.

My chemo week starts with a high-energy sleepless night because of the steroid given intravenously before the two chemo drugs. The chemotherapy drugs produce a laundry list of symptoms that lasts through the first week: nausea, fatigue, poor sleep, constipation, acne, and burning mouth, nose and eyes. I get bleeding from my nose, mouth and anus and cracks in my dry skin that can take a couple months to heal. The sore mouth (mucositis) is my worst symptom and is slowly improving at the end of three weeks, only to be assaulted by another course of chemotherapy. If I were at the very end of my life, I wouldn't continue on this chemotherapy. The side effects wouldn't be worth the benefit.

In an unusual twist of fate, I am thankful for my mucosits. My mouth is always sore, especially when I eat. Most people on my kind of chemotherapy don't suffer from mucositis to the degree that I do. Yet, it was the severity of my mucosits that caused me to change from weekly chemotherapy to taking it only every three weeks. If that had not occurred, I would be taking my chemotherapy weekly. My fatigue would have never left. I would never have the experience of two weeks forward and one week back that characterizes my three-week chemo cycle.

God works in strange and mysterious ways. I know of many people who are confident that they know how God had answered their prayers. I don't necessarily share their confidence. I know that God's will is done. God is powerful enough that I believe His will is carried out whether I pray or not. God changes me when I pray. The change is a spiritual one that is good for my soul. I believe that we give God too little credit for our lives and the world around us. We can easily take God's creation for granted as it is so interwoven into our lives. We ask for more and fail to appreciate all that God does. I could complain that my mouth is sore but then have to admit that my life on chemotherapy is much better because of my mucositis which led to my receiving chemotherapy every three weeks instead of weekly. This is an answer to prayer that has not gone unappreciated.

I would like to be rid of my cancer, chronic pain, and all the other side effects that I have suffered from its treatment. That would be a home run. Instead, I have singled, stole second base and, whether it is on earth or in heaven, I am in scoring position. I praise God for giving me a life that I never dreamed would exist when my chemotherapy started last May.

I want to revel in the belief that good things are happening in my life because I have been good enough to receive God's special favor. I want to think that God has granted me a second chance at life with great results on chemotherapy because God needs me on earth for a longer period of time. I would like to believe that God's mind was changed by all the prayers offered to Him for healing and a cure. Yet I can't read the Bible and believe that any of this is true. Instead I will remain impressed that my body is poisoned every three weeks by chemotherapy, and then my body heals and regenerates in that three-week interval before we inflict the next round of chemo. God's healing hand is there, tucked into our rudimentary understandings of biology and healing. It is a miracle of healing that doesn't place me at the center of God's universe.

I am not bold enough to say that my understanding of how God works through prayer is correct. God certainly has the ability to perform curative miracles of healing. In humility, though, I must admit that my earthly life isn't so highly valued that God will keep me here longer than my biologic clock has been programmed.

I should be able to live under the knowledge that God has already shown His grace, offered His son, and given me a new life. It shouldn't surprise me if God doesn't produce a miraculous cure for my cancer. It should surprise me that, in my sinful world, God hasn't given up on me. That should be enough.

***

What does "God works in mysterious ways" mean to you?

In what ways has God answered your prayers for healing?

46. CPR is lifesaving: Fact or fiction?

April 30, 2015

One year ago, I put on my Do Not Resuscitate (DNR) bracelet. For Amy and me, it wasn't a difficult decision. My tongue cancer had spread, I was terminally ill, had lost weight, and was in pain. I realized that if I had the opportunity to die suddenly, it would be a better death than what appeared to be in store for me. I also knew that as my health was deteriorating, the chance that CPR could successfully bring me back to a normal life was almost nil.

CPR can be a great lifesaving procedure. But for some, it also has a dark side of creating prolonged agony before death. CPR is initiated when a person stops breathing or the heart stops beating. In the 1960s, when our current CPR protocols were developed with rescue breathing and chest compressions, it was found to be lifesaving primarily for those who had suffered a witnessed heart attack. Outside of the hospital, if a bystander immediately administered CPR, it improved your chance of survival. The general public and the medical profession developed high expectations for CPR.

Television programming has served only to amplify those high expectations. One study showed that 75% of all CPR shown on TV is successful in resuscitating the patient. The patient returns to normal life 67% of the time. The patients are often young, and the results are dramatic, perfect for a television episode.

What are the real life statistics? A Japanese study of 95,000 times when bystanders witnessed a cardiac arrest and CPR was performed outside of the hospital showed that only 8% survived one month. Perhaps more troubling was the finding that a paltry 3% returned to a normal life while 3% were left in a vegetative state. Another study looked at sixty-nine patients who were terminally ill, had DNR ordered but still received CPR. Only 11% survived, but none lived for 48 hours. The true success rate was 0%.

When I started my family medicine residency over thirty years ago, the first day of our program began with an Acute Cardiac Life Support course. The course was important because, as medical residents, we were expected to participate in all Code Blues that occurred in the hospital. A Code Blue was called when a patient stopped breathing or his heart stopped beating. We would run quickly through the hospital to the patient's room. I remember one of my first codes where I arrived and began chest compressions. The patient was a frail and petite elderly woman, and I did everything according to protocol. I heard and felt her ribs crack as I placed the weight of my upper body through my hands onto her upper chest. I was relieved that she didn't survive; I wondered how much pain she would have felt from her broken ribs, had she awoken.

CPR has its place. It can be an absolutely lifesaving procedure for a healthy person suffering a heart attack. For a weak and frail elderly person or person in declining health because of a terminal illness, it is often best to forego this procedure. Do Not Resuscitate is slowly undergoing a name change to Allow Natural Death (AND). The hope is that patients will not view a DNR order as a withholding of life extending treatment. Allow Natural Death puts a more positive spin on a decision to forego CPR when the end result is not likely to be good.

I received a phone call in early January from Dr. Jim Deming, my palliative care specialist. He knew that my health had improved to the point where I had signed up to run a 100- mile race. He said, "Dave, I think it might be time to cut off your DNR bracelet." As Amy cut off my DNR bracelet, it reminded me that much of life is uncertain. While there was no question that I needed a DNR bracelet in May of last year, it had now become equally obvious that I would want CPR if I suffered a heart attack and needed resuscitation in Arizona. When my cancer returns, my pain intensifies, and my health is in decline, I will be quick to put on another DNR bracelet.

All of us should consider the facts in determining if a DNR order is right for you. Let's not use TV shows as our guide.

***

At what point in your life would you want to wear a Do Not Resuscitate bracelet? What factors would have to be considered?

What did you think of the statistics of survival after bystander CPR (3%)?

What is the difference, in your mind, between 'Do not resuscitate,' and 'Allow natural death?'

47. A moral compass

May 7, 2015

Amy and I have been blessed with two great sons. But quite honestly, we never knew how our children would turn out while they were growing up. The road to adulthood included the risk of hazardous wrong turns and misdirection. As they grew older, there were many other influences in their lives. We watched them falter at times but trusted that they would develop into more resilient adults because of it.

Children aren't born with instruction manuals on how to raise them. Parents can wander through a forest of trial and error but often end up taking the same path of childrearing trod by their own parents. Young children constantly test parents, work to expand their limits, and manipulate us to get their way. The challenges grow with time. Little children, little problems: Big children, big problems.

I find it interesting that when we talk to others about our children, we talk about what they do. Nathan is a mechanical engineer in Texas, going back to grad school, has a steady girlfriend, and likes to hunt. Eric is a chemistry graduate student in Iowa, getting married next week to a wonderful woman, and likes to play ultimate Frisbee and chess. These descriptions are superficial. If I were to tell you that I am proud to be the father of these two young men, it would not be for the reasons listed above. It would be because of their character.

When I think back to their years growing up and ask myself what were some of my proudest moments, I remember some quirky stories. Each one is a story about their character. In today's society, stories of character might be construed as bragging. So these are stories that are rarely told.

I remember camping with another family who had younger kids. We were loading up each child with an armful of firewood. A younger child was upset that he couldn't carry as much as the bigger kids. Nathan was quick to give him the same number of sticks as the big kids; he just cleverly used smaller ones. The young child felt helpful and proud. Nathan once sent a neighbor boy home after the kid was mean to Eric; he was standing up for his little brother. We are appreciative that at Christmastime, instead of giving us a gift, he finds a charity or needy individual who is grateful for his donation. Nathan happily pitches in with projects around the house and often works beside me. He is a hard worker who never whines or complains.

Eric once sat with a younger kindergarten child on the school bus who had vomited and was embarrassed. While other kids were grossed out, Eric moved over to sit with him to reassure and comfort him. His mother called to tell us the story and tearfully thanked us. As a teenager Eric once anonymously slipped $500 into the purse of a friend's mother. The father was unemployed, and the family was struggling. He would need to work about seventy hours at his job at Marketplace Foods to earn $500, but he had no reservations about donating his money. He had a knack for making less popular kids feel welcome and never liked seeing anyone feel excluded. While on vacation at Disney, Eric noticed a young man sitting alone at the edge of the pool. He went over to sit with him and struck up a conversation. It was apparent that the young man had autism, but he clearly enjoyed the attention.

We don't talk about our children's character like we talk about their schooling, jobs, activities and relationships. Parental success in our society seems to be measured by our children's achievements in the classroom, the athletic field, and the working world. Our children, now in their 20s, have more access to guidance on how to apply for further schooling, launch a career, create wealth, or find a mate than on how to develop inner qualities like kindness, honesty, generosity, sacrifice, gratitude, compassion, peace, and love. As parents, we want our children to develop a Christian faith that cultivates an inner spiritual self, a character that will provide them with a moral compass for life. We hope and pray that the rest of their lives are guided by that character. Education is a road to being able to serve others, careers become a calling, and relationships are filled with unconditional love. In a sometimes dark and competitive world, we want our children to shine as a light of collaboration and assistance to others.

I approach the end of life with great peace, believing that our children have developed a Christian-centered moral compass to lead them through life. I appreciate that I was healthy and present during those crucial child-rearing years. They are now independent adults and able to make it on their own. Our children give me one more reason to believe that I have received more blessings in this life than I have earned or deserve.

"WE SWELL WITH PRIDE WHEN THOSE WE LOVE DO WELL. BUT OUR HEARTS ARE WARMED WHEN THOSE WE LOVE DO GOOD."   -Rev. Gordon Long

***

How do children learn moral values?

What would you want said at your eulogy? How would it be different than your curriculum vitae?

48. The outlier

May 12, 2015

Amy and I just spent a long day at the Mayo Clinic in Rochester, MN. It had been one year since I last saw my head and neck surgeon and ENT oncologist. One year ago, my tongue cancer had spread to distant areas of my body. It was expected that I would not need to return to Mayo in Rochester since my prognosis was poor. My local oncologist, palliative care physician, and family doc could handle end-of-life care.

Yesterday's PET scan showed a remarkable and unexpected improvement in my cancer. All of the cancer areas that lit up on the scan last year in my neck, chest, and skin have disappeared. There remains a large area, however, that is still of concern. I have a sore in the floor of my mouth that has slowly enlarged over the past year. It is an area of necrosis (rotted dead flesh) that travels from the floor of my mouth under my tongue and into the jaw bone. At this time it can't be determined if this area is just cancer that has died or if there may be some active cancer remaining.

The head and neck surgeon cleaned out dead jawbone that is exposed in the floor of my mouth in an effort to encourage this area of osteonecrosis to heal. We discussed the possibility of surgery that would cut out all of the abnormal area on the PET scan, but the consequences of this extensive surgery would be severe. It would negatively affect speech and swallowing and leave me with a wound that may not heal. We decided not to pursue this option.

Instead, we will first see if there is any cancer in the dead bone that was removed from my jawbone yesterday. If no cancer is seen in this dead bone, we will discontinue chemotherapy. Over time, my mouth will change in one of two ways. If the open sore enlarges, my jaw becomes more painful, or the cancerous skin nodules return, then we will biopsy to confirm that cancer is still present. I will return to my previous chemotherapy which hopefully would be successful again. If the jawbone and open sore in my mouth heals, then it would suggest that the cancer is gone. Being off chemotherapy will encourage the area to heal if no cancer is present.

I don't know if people really understand how unlikely it is to be cured of an advanced and recurrent head and neck cancer. Many people may have a friend or relative who "beat cancer" and, therefore, don't appreciate how rare it is to have someone in my situation survive cancer-free. My ENT oncologist, who sees only ear, nose and throat cancers, said that if it turns out that the cancer doesn't return, it would be "one in a million." My head and neck surgeon was no less dramatic. He said that if this is a cure, "we will be talking about you 10-15 years from now." Neither of them could believe that all of the areas on the PET scan that previously showed an extensive spread of cancer had now cleared. Neither of them thought I would be alive today. I am truly an outlier; statistically this should not be happening.

I have been known to say that there are two things that you never want in life. You don't want to be the headline story on the evening news, and you don't want to be a famous patient at the Mayo Clinic. I guess that I will have to retract the last half of that statement. Today, I would be thrilled to be famous at the Mayo Clinic.

How do you explain the unexplainable? Did I have an exceptional response to my chemotherapy? I had significant side effects from my chemotherapy which can be a sign that it will be more effective. Did my good lifestyle habits make a difference? I am physically fit. Even when I was weak and wasted last summer, I never gave up on walking and regular exercise. I eat a healthy diet that includes many servings of fruits and vegetables every day. Yet these were health habits that I had practiced my whole life. The only health habit change I've made is that I rest now when I am tired. I don't push from sunup to sundown which was always my mode of operation in the past. Maybe my immune system has benefited from more sleep, rest and relaxation.

Is it prayer? I have posted before that we should always credit God for any healing that occurs. I don't really care if it was chemotherapy or good health habits that contributed to a spectacular result. If I ever lose sight of God's healing hand in all of this, then I have reached a point where the Great Healer hasn't received his due. Even when I have boldly announced that I don't pray for a cure, I know that God's will is done and that healing is in God's domain. It is time to thank all of you who have prayed and asked for God's healing hand to intervene. My family and I are grateful.

We still don't know when or if my cancer will rear its ugly head. We do know that I have been blessed with an additional year of life that was not expected. Our son Eric and his fiancée Sarah will be married in Menomonie this Saturday. They were engaged last October. Sarah's mother Margie suggested that Eric and Sarah move up the wedding to last December so that I could attend. Bless her heart. It was a lovely request. I intervened and said that marriage is a decision that is so important that plans for a wedding date shouldn't be changed based on my health. I said, "Let's trust God that it will all work out." The kids set their date as May 16, accepting that we could not control or predict the future. I am delighted that I can be present as father of the groom and welcome Sarah into our family.

I don't know what the future will bring, but in life there is always room for hope and optimism. Thanks be to God for the miracle of life.

REJOICE ALWAYS, PRAY CONSTANTLY, GIVE THANKS IN ALL CIRCUMSTANCES; FOR THIS IS THE WILL OF GOD IN CHRIST JESUS FOR YOU."   I Thessalonians 5: 16-18

***

What is your biggest motivator to live longer?

How do you define 'miracle'?

49. Next leg of the journey

May 20, 2015

These last two years of living with cancer have been the most transformative years of my adult life. There is nothing like facing your own mortality to help clarify what is important in life and what is just trivial background noise. One year ago, death seemed to be closing in on me at an alarming speed. I still remember putting on my once skin-tight bike shorts only to see them draped loosely over my withered body. I remember suffering so much pain in my jaw that I almost didn't start on the chemotherapy that led to the rampant destruction of my body's cancer cells. I recall sleeping with a CPAP breathing machine so I could feel somewhat rested the next morning. I spent months eating only pureed foods and drinking liquids because it was too painful to chew.

Although these are becoming more distant memories, my life will never be the same. I started weekly journal entries in CaringBridge anticipating that my time left on earth would be short. I wanted to stay connected with patients who I had grown close to over the previous twenty-seven years as a family physician. I didn't schedule a final retirement reception for patients and community members at that time. I knew that such a gathering would be too emotional for me. CaringBridge provided a means of communication that could include family and friends as well as patients.

I changed as a person over the last two years. I became more reflective about life and all the events that precede death. Some themes emerged, and I wanted to share those stories and themes with others. I was somewhat disheartened that because of HIPAA patient confidentiality rules, I couldn't share some of the greatest stories that I have experienced in life. I learned how to live at life's end from my patients. Many were heroic at the end of life. They were a calming presence to family and friends. Even when faced with issues of pain, weakness, and dependence at life's end, they thrived. They found joy in relationships. They led their families through a grieving process with smiles, hugs, and endearing words of conversation.

Perhaps the most important lesson to share is that we can find hope and joy even when the headwinds of life are blowing strong. Those headwinds come in everyone's life. We endure those headwinds when we shelter ourselves by huddling together against them. To live with Amy through this storm has strengthened our bond of marriage. When those marriage vows of "in sickness or in health" become dominated by sickness, you really find out who you married. I found a woman who has decided that helping me to live a better life is not just on her radar; it is a life goal. I am indebted to her care and love shown over the course of the last two years.

In my situation, the best way to approach cancer was to reduce it to background noise. It was always present, but I wouldn't allow it to consume my thoughts and energy. There were many times when I felt ill from the cancer or treatment and decided to do the things that bring joy to life. Amy and I sought to live life as fully as possible. I was committed to not leaving this world with "he lost the battle with cancer" in my obituary. You don't lose a battle against background noise.

I don't know what the future holds. The next leg of the journey is unclear. People are now asking if I will be back at work. Although I would like to return, I won't be quick to declare myself cancer-free. I still have a large open sore in my mouth and necrotic areas in my jaw that need to heal. I still wear a narcotic pain patch that has been indispensable in my ability to enjoy life. I will be ready to return to active employment when these two issues are resolved.

Because my recovery has been so unexpected and unusual, there is no longer a prognosis. Unlike every other stage of my cancer, we now have no idea what is the likelihood that my cancer will return. If it does return, I will still be a happy man. I have received a level of health and a new lease on life that no one, not even I, thought possible. Amy and I saw our son Eric marry the love of his life last weekend. We live for events and days like this. But we are also more aware and appreciate all the mundane and everyday joys: running with friends, working outside in beautiful weather, getting a full night's sleep. I have been blessed with a life that has been given new legs.

I hope that all of us can ponder life more deeply and explore the reason why we occupy earth for this short time. I needed the rigors of cancer treatment and days away from work to peer more deeply into the soul of life. We easily become overly engrossed in the business of daily life. We lose track of purpose and meaning. We can live life as if we were a business that never developed a mission or vision statement. My hope is that the stories I have told in CaringBridge over the past year will inspire. We live well when life is not about ourselves but is centered on others.

Finally, my hope is that the headwinds of life serve to strengthen our faith in God. I realize that I have lived a privileged life. I wouldn't trade my life for anyone else's life. Living with cancer hasn't destroyed my gratitude for this great life. God has been good to Amy and me even through a tough journey with cancer. While we can't fully appreciate heaven, there is peacefulness in knowing that God has promised a better life that awaits our arrival.

I have posted fifty CaringBridge journal entries this past year. It has helped me to clarify what is important in my life. I feel honored that readers have found my personal thoughts and stories helpful in their own lives. I hope that it has inspired others to live a better life. My plan is to quit journaling weekly. I will still occasionally post an update on my health and continued journey with cancer. God's blessings to you and your family. Live well.

IF GOD SENDS YOU DOWN A STONY PATH, MAY HE GIVE YOU STRONG SHOES.   −Irish saying

***

What gives your life purpose and meaning?

In what ways have you served someone as caregiver? Have you had a need for someone to care for you through a long illness?

50. An unwelcome invader returns

August 22, 2015

Amy and I just came back from the Mayo Clinic in Rochester yesterday. I have a condition called osteoradionecrosis (ORN) of the mandible (jawbone). It is a complication caused by the head and neck radiation that I received in the fall of 2013. The radiation destroyed the blood supply to my left mandible which now has been slowly disintegrating. It also produced an open sore in the floor of my mouth that harbors a foul smelling and foul tasting drainage. It makes eating painful.

The necrotic wound in my mouth has slowly enlarged over the past fifteen months. Since my cancer was so widespread in May of 2014, it didn't make any sense to try to fix the problem. The cancer was ultimately going to be a much larger problem. After having a PET scan in May of 2015 that showed resolution of the metastatic cancer areas, we decided that it was time to address the ORN.

For the past five weeks, I have been undergoing a variety of treatments to enhance healing and prep me for upcoming surgery. Five days per week, I lie in a hyperbaric oxygen chamber to help build new blood vessels. I take a daily intravenous antibiotic to clear any infection out of the bone. I am on a number of additional medications as well. The plan was to undergo surgery to scrape out any of the dead bone in my jaw and dead flesh in my mouth.

The pain in my tongue, jaw and mouth has increased steadily over the last six weeks. Six weeks ago, I spent a week at the Rob Krar Ultrarunning Camp in Flagstaff, AZ. I was able to eat most foods and run mountain trails. I was on a small amount of pain medicine at that time but was starting to need more pain relief. By the time I saw my surgeon yesterday to discuss upcoming surgery, the pain and amount of pain medication that I am taking has gone up significantly. The other two times when I had pain like this, it was because of cancer. By the end of the visit yesterday, we knew that this pain was again due to the recurrence of cancer.

A firm nodule on my tongue was biopsied and came back positive for cancer. This changed all of our plans. We scheduled CT scans of the head and neck, a PET scan to look for distant metastases, and a return visit to my oncologist. By the end of next week, we should know our next steps. There are now multiple surgical options for dealing with the ORN of the mandible and the newly biopsied cancer. The scans will show how far the cancer has extended and will influence the surgical decision.

It is likely that I will end up back on chemotherapy. I had great results last year on Erbitux and Taxol so I suspect that these will be used again. Despite the bad news and increasing pain, this year has been better than I ever could have imagined. I went to my fortieth year high school class reunion on a riverboat last weekend. We also spent part of the weekend attending the Luther Park Quilt Auction. More surgery and more chemo lie ahead but are just bumps in the road. We know how to navigate road bumps.

I will have more details about my treatment course after this Wednesday's scans and visits. As always thanks in advance for your prayers, concern, and friendship.

***

Discuss ways in which 'hindsight is 50/50' have been true in your life. What decisions would you have made differently?

What are some strategies you use to navigate the 'bumps in the road' of your life?

51. Back on chemo

September 4, 2015

We had some favorable news last week. The PET scan showed that the tongue cancer has returned in the tongue and a larger area below the tongue with only one lymph node involved. That is considerably less cancer than I had with my last recurrence in May of 2014. My oncologist thinks that the increased pain that I am experiencing is primarily from cancer and not from osteoradionecrosis of the mandible. The bottom line is that I went back on chemotherapy one week ago, and we are holding off on jaw surgery for now. Last year, the chemotherapy was very effective, and I stayed on it for a year. We are hopeful that the chemotherapy will be equally effective this time around.

It is hard to believe that less than two months ago I was running 11-12 miles per day on mountain trails in Northern Arizona. Now I haven't run for several weeks as my mouth has become progressively more painful. I am losing weight since it hurts to eat. I am at my lowest weight since being first diagnosed with cancer. This week, I am nauseous from chemotherapy and unable to regain any weight. I feel weak. It is amazing how quickly life with cancer can go from a high to a low.

My biggest issue is chronic pain. In a little over one month, I increased my fentanyl pain patch from 6mcg to 50mcg. This isn't enough narcotic to control the pain so I am regularly taking additional morphine during the day. I put a local anesthetic on the open wound in my mouth right before eating pureed or liquid foods. I have used physical exercise, guided imagery and prayer to relieve pain. I have seen a physical therapist for neck exercises, and have used massage, heat and even acupuncture. My best success has come from medications prescribed by my family physician. It also has been helpful to see a pain and palliative care specialist who has offered some good medication options for treating pain and some of the narcotic side effects.

This escalation in pain has a significant effect on my life. I sleep poorly at night and nap in the afternoons. I spend about 12-14 hours per day in bed to try to cobble together adequate sleep. It is more difficult to enjoy life. The narcotic pain relievers cause poor appetite, nausea, constipation, poor sleep and fatigue. The narcotics can reduce the pain but never takes it completely away.

The surgery incision on the inside of my mouth is now sixteen months old. It has never healed and continues to grow. It makes eating and talking painful. My jaw is painful from radiation damage (osteoradionecrosis). It is just a matter of time before some major dental issues erupt because of the damaged bone. Surgery on my jaw will be required in the future. My neck muscles are tight and sore from surgery and radiation. I just started back on chemotherapy and am developing mucositis (mouth soreness). All of this collateral damage in treating cancer makes life less comfortable.

It has always seemed that cancer specialists are most interested in curing patients and less interested in dealing with the aftermath of their treatments. My head and neck surgeon has suggested surgery as an option to remove all of the cancer that can be seen on PET scan. A surgery that extensive would permanently change my ability to talk and swallow. Some things in life are worse than death. Neither Amy nor I have any desire to keep cutting out parts of my mouth and tongue as we chase a growing cancer.

Cancer patients who are cured often live with side effects from the cancer treatments, pain being the most common. It has been reported that 60-85% of all cancer survivors live with pain. It is a testament to the harshness of our current cancer treatments. Ultimately, half of all cancer patients still suffer with pain that goes undertreated. That doesn't come as a surprise, knowing that we build up tolerance to narcotic pain relievers over time so progressively larger doses may be needed to control pain.

Most physicians readily believe cancer patients who report living with chronic pain. The doctors believe me, and my family physician who prescribes my narcotic pain relievers has not made me sign a narcotics medication contract or subjected me to urine drug screens to receive opioids. I alter my dosing according to my level of pain and am trusted to do this. I use as little narcotic pain reliever as possible, knowing that I don't want to build up tolerance. Yet when my cancer returned, it has been absolutely necessary to increase my dose of narcotics to have any hope of enjoying life. I live with empathy for those who suffer with chronic pain. I wish that all patients who live with chronic pain could be trusted and treated with the same dignity that I have experienced.

"Pain insists upon being attended to. God whispers to us in our pleasures, speaks in our consciences, but shouts in our pains. It is his megaphone to rouse a deaf world."

C. S. Lewis

***

What experience do you have with dealing with chronic pain, either yourself, or someone close to you?

What are the advantages to experiencing suffering?

52. A time to live and a time to die

December 6, 2015

I haven't felt significantly hungry for months. The combination of an oral cancer, and taking in progressively larger doses of narcotic pain relievers, contribute to my lack of appetite. It is part of the dying process. Over the years, it had been common for me to hear from a patient approaching death that they have very little desire to eat. Meanwhile, their family members are pulling out every favorite dish or dessert in a desperate attempt to prevent the inevitable weight loss that precedes death.

For months now, I have been trying to eat more calories to maintain my weight. Even though I don't have an appetite, I have been forcing myself to eat in the hope that I can make one more return to the health that I enjoyed earlier this year. Unfortunately, the pain isn't improving this time around. The mouth wound continues to grow in size. I am losing strength even as my weight stays steady. There are many signs that the chemotherapy isn't working to improve the physical and emotional recovery I experienced last year. I really haven't been able to enjoy life with my current level of pain. If I take enough pain relievers to feel comfortable, I become groggy and wobbly on my feet. If I consistently take enough narcotics to control my pain, then I will eventually build-up a tolerance to them. I will require more medication to attain the same amount of relief. It has been a challenge to balance pain control, and the side effects of narcotic use.

How much pain should I allow myself to tolerate? When I am no longer enjoying life because of pain and/or side effects from the pain relievers, then the answer comes into a much clearer focus. It now is very painful to eat and to talk. Before eating, I use a special numbing medication that I swish in my mouth to help lessen the pain, but still often struggle to finish my meals of liquids and pureed foods. When visiting with others, I try to minimize talking by having my wife Amy at my side to talk for me. She does a great job of diverting speaking away from me.

When I have reached a point where pain or narcotic side effects are always present, and the hope for recovery from this state has dissipated, then it is time to let nature take its course.

What is nature's course? It is what I have already been experiencing for months. I have no appetite. It is a natural process that allows us to lose our appetite at the end of life. There are no uncomfortable hunger pangs. There is no desire to eat. If we simply follow our body's desire to stop eating, it brings us toward death, and allows an escape from pain or other sufferings that have been part of the illness.

There is a time to live and a time to die. Determining when to make that transition has been the most difficult ethical question in my journey with cancer. I can continue to fight the process of dying by consuming more calories than my body desires. This could prolong my life, but it is doubtful that it would improve the quality of my life. I could also choose to continue taking chemotherapy every three weeks, in the hopes that the treatment would provide some relief from pain, as it did last year. It appears that I have reached the point of diminished returns, when it comes to chemo. Chemotherapy is not improving the quality of my life.

Now that states are passing "Right to Die" laws that allow physician-assisted suicide, the options of how to die are looking more skewed. We should be passing laws that strengthen hospice and palliative care programs. We should protect medical providers, hospice nurses and family members from being sued or criminally charged when their actions of giving large doses of pain medication to ease pain were well-intended. In Belgium and the Netherlands, where more than one out of thirty citizens now die through physician-assisted suicide, the hospice movement has been dismally slow to gain a foothold. My

fear is that in states with physician-assisted
many terminally ill patients will believe that
two options: an assisted death, or living wit
suffering.

Last week, we had appointments in Rocheste
treatment options, and to tweak pain control medications.
We have decided that it is time to discontinue
chemotherapy, as it is not working, and, in fact, making life
more uncomfortable. We are going to be meeting with the
hospice department to set up services from those
professionals. So while this is a big decision, it is one in
which we are comfortable. We have always known this day
would come. And we are very grateful that this day has
been delayed by many months.

Once again, we thank you for your friendship and
continued supportive prayers and love. We are blessed
beyond measure.

Peace be with you.

"For everything there is a season, and a time for every
matter under heaven: a time to be born, and a time to die;
a time to weep, and a time to laugh; a time to mourn, and
a time to dance;"   Ecclesiastes 3: 1-2, 4

***

Living and dying are a natural part of life. Why do we
sometimes fight death so vigorously?

What are your thoughts on states passing 'right to die'
laws, and physician-assisted suicide? What are the
advantages/disadvantages to having an option for
assisted suicide? Under what circumstances would
you consider assisted suicide?

Epilogue

David C. Eitrheim, M.D. completed the race of his life, crossing the finish line on January 1, 2016, at home, surrounded by family. Finishing time was 58 years 8 months 9 days.

Running is life

Oh, the thousands of miles! Of time spent in holy space. Oh, the joy of endless discussions on life's issues such as medicine, faith, politics, ethics and of course running-nerd talk - new and old races, training, this or that new thing, and the importance and joy of new running shoes! Of free medical opinions, but better keep on moving.

Running becomes a paradigm of life, of friendship, camaraderie, adventure, and challenge. It is Dave who showed us these things and together became the life we would share on the trail or the road in heat, wind, snow, rain, in forest and mountain, dawn and dusk, and miles of city streets.

Running was Sabbath. It is for us a sacred time apart, to renew, to reflect and to share the unspoken silence of creation with only the steady rhythm of breath and footfalls. Running was therapy. It was a time to support one another in our weakness and to console each other in our failures, sealed with the absolution of unquestioned friendship.

Running is destiny. Running so many miles and not really having a good reason as to why - because we can or are we just a bit crazy? Running to a destiny, which is always over the next hill, around the next corner or just living to run another day as destiny waits. But not really knowing where it will all end; only fearing that it will.

So, we run into a future that is only God's, a destiny that is sure, but such a mystery. We console ourselves with it, but the loneliness of one less set of feet on this journey will be ever present.

We are so blessed to have Dave on this incredible journey. Let us run and not be weary. To run again in some great beyond, running in the joy of resurrection and life and running that will never end. Running is life. Thank you, Dave! ~R.M.

"... They shall run and not be weary, they shall walk and not faint." Isaiah 40:31

Running Career Statistics: Over 40,000 miles run since 1980; First Marathon: 1976; Fastest Marathon: 2:51; 91 Marathons; 36 Ultramarathons -14 were 100-milers; Favorite Marathon: Grandma's Marathon (ran 25 times)

David was born in Tyler MN on April 23, 1957 to Norman and Clarice (Pederson) Eitrheim. He was baptized into the death and life of Christ on May 10, 1957 at First English Lutheran Church in Tyler MN. The family moved to Fridley MN when Dave was five. He graduated from Fridley High School in 1975 and was valedictorian of his class.

Dave is a graduate of Augsburg College, and the University of Minnesota Medical School in Duluth and Minneapolis. He trained at the Sioux Falls South Dakota Family Medicine Residency Program and joined the staff of Red Cedar Clinic in Menomonie in 1987, serving as a member of the governing board as Red Cedar later became part of the Mayo Clinic Health System.

Dave's interest in medicine and work as a physician included the entire spectrum of life, from delivering hundreds of newborns and following those children as they grew up, to being present and caring for others as they died. He provided clinic and emergency room care, as well as inpatient hospital and nursing home care for thousands of people. As an advocate for social justice, he volunteered regularly at the Free Clinic of the Greater Menomonie Area. His devotion to his medical practice and community was honored in 2004 when he was named Family Physician of the Year by the Wisconsin Academy of Family Physicians.

Dave's leadership in medicine has been demonstrated locally in a number of areas: In the early 1990s Dave volunteered as Medical Director to develop the first hospice program in Dunn County. As an avid teacher, in 1998 Dave led the development of the Menomonie Rural Training track Family Medicine Residency Program. He taught students and residents from Duluth, Madison and Rochester for over two decades.

As a regional and national leader in Family Medicine, Dave served on the Board of the Wisconsin Academy of Family Physicians and was named president in 2014. He led a number of initiatives important to family physicians, including nationally acclaimed work in office efficiency, team-based care and the Patient Centered Medical Home. He was a founding member of the Quality Review Board of the Mayo Clinic.

To his colleagues Dave was known as a mentor and friend. A physician of great knowledge, expertise and integrity, he could always be consulted for the latest medical information and technique, knowing that for him, the interest of the patient was the only interest to be considered. For thousands of people in West Central Wisconsin over the last three decades, that knowledge, expertise and integrity were best experienced in a simple office visit. There, his warm heart and clinical expertise and genuine caring would influence many to improved health, and ultimately saved countless lives. ~M.D.-S

Dave is survived by his wife of 33 years Amy Jo Eitrheim (Kaste) of Menomonie, their sons Nathan David of College Station TX, and Eric Steven (Sarah) of Iowa City IA, parents Norman and Clarice (Pederson) Eitrheim of Sioux Falls SD, brother Daniel (Patricia) Eitrheim of Bloomington MN, brother John (Stephanie)Eitrheim of Austin TX, and sister Marie (Bob) Feely of Minneapolis, as well as numerous in-laws, aunts, uncles, cousins, nieces, nephews, friends, colleagues, patients, and running buddies. To say he will be missed is an enormous understatement.

Cited Works

Chapter 13
Near-death experience. Wikipedia, November 9, 2015.

Chapter 14
Cancer Facts and Figures 2015. Cancer.org/acs. Website.

Chapter 15

NOVA: MD - The Making of a Doctor. Run time 120 minutes. Movie.

2013 Annual Survey. WAFP.org. Website.

Chapter 18

Mukherjee, Siddhartha. *The Emperor of All Maladies: A Biography of Cancer.* (2010) Scribner and Sons

Chapter 19

Turner, Kelly A. PhD. *Radical Remission: Surviving Cancer Against All Odds.* (2014) Harper Collins

Chapter 23

"If you could change one thing about your body, what would that be?" Jubilee Project, October 29, 2015. YouTube video.

Chapter 24

Franks, P., and K. Fiscella. 1998. "Primary Care Physicians and Specialists as Personal Physicians: Health Care Expenditures and Mortality Experience." *Journal of Family Practice* 47(2): 105–109.

Baicker, K., and A. Chandra. 2004. "Medicare Spending, the Physician Workforce, and Beneficiaries' Quality of Care." *Health Affairs* 23:w184–w197 (published online 7 April 2004).

Chapter 27

http://www.csmonitor.com/Commentary/Editorial-Board-Blog/2010/0910/Gallup-poll-Degree-of-one-s-charity-depends-on-happiness-more-than-wealth

Chapter 28

Gawande, A. (2014) *Being mortal.* New York, New York: Henry Holt and Co.

Chapter 34

Jerry Seinfeld quote:
http://www.goodreads.com/quotes/162599-according-to-most-studies-people-s-number-one-fear-is-public

Robin Williams quote:
http://www.bustle.com/articles/35405-11-robin-williams-dead-poets-society-quotes-that-will-inspire-you-to-carpe-diem

Chapter 35

Dave Barry quote:
http://www.goodreads.com/quotes/107949-skiing-combines-outdoor-fun-with-knocking-down-trees-with-your

Chapter 40

http://www.honeyfoundation.org/learn/research-info/

CHAPTER 42

JENNIFER S TEMEL ET AL., "EARLY PALLIATIVE CARE FOR PATIENTS WITH METASTATIC NON-SMALL-CELL LUNG CANCER," *NEW ENGLAND JOURNAL OF MEDICINE* 363(8) (AUGUST 19, 2010): 733-42.

S R CONNOR ET AL., "COMPARING HOSPICE AND NONHOSPICE PATIENT SURVIVAL AMONG PATIENTS WHO DIE WITHIN A THREE-YEAR WINDOW," *JOURNAL OF PAIN AND SYMPTOM MANAGEMENT* 33(3) (MARCH 2007): 238-46.

Gawande, A. (2014) *Being mortal.* New York, New York: Henry Holt and Co.

Chapter 43

Alexi A Wright et al., "Associations between end-of-life discussions, patient mental health, medical care near death, and caregiver bereavement adjustment," *Journal of the American Medical Association* 300(14) (October 8, 2008): 1665-73.

Chapter 44

William J. Mayo, MD, Rush Medical College Commencement, 1910Thomas R Viggiano et al., "Putting the needs of the patient first: Mayo Clinic's core value, institutional culture, and professionalism covenant," *Academic Medicine* 82(11) (November 2007): 1089-93.

Chapter 46

SJ Diem, JD Lantos, JA Tulsky, "Cardiopulmonary Resuscitation on Television. Miracles and Misinformation," *New England Journal of Medicine* 334(24) (June 13, 1996): 1578-82.

Hideo Yasunaga, "Collaborative Effects of Bystander-Initiated Cardiopulmonary Resuscitation and Prehospital Advanced Cardiac Life Support by Physicians on Survival of Out-of-Hospital Cardiac Arrest: A Nationwide Population-Based Observational Study," *Critical Care* 14(6) (November 4, 2010): R199.

C H Wise et al, "Prehospital Emergency Treatment of Palliative Care Patients with Cardiac Arrest: A Retroactive Investigation," *Supportive Care in Cancer* 18(10) (October 2010): 1287-92.

Chapter 51

"A Nation in Pain: Healing Our Biggest Health Problem" by Judy Foreman, Oxford UniversityPress 2014

Chronology

July 2013- Diagnosed with squamous cell carcinoma of the tongue (stage IVa); surgery to remove tumor, and lymph node resection

September 2013- Start of weekly chemotherapy and radiation treatments

October 2013- End of chemotherapy and radiation treatments

December 2013- Vacation to Florida/ Disney World!

January 2013- Returns to medical practice full time

February 2014- PET scan shows no signs of cancer; Ski vacation in Colorado

Early May 2014- Increase pain, salivary gland surgically removed as possible source of pain

Late May 2014- Cancer returns explaining the increased pain, terminal prognosis (9 months), start palliative chemotherapy. Retires from medical practice

June 2014- Start of CaringBridge posts

July 2014- Ran July 4th 5k with son, needed to walk the hills

November 2014- Rails to Trails Marathon in Wisconsin

December 2014- Vacation with friends in Florida

January 2015- Vacation in Arizona and ran 60 miles of 100 mile race; skied for a week in Steamboat Springs, Colorado

May 2015- Ran half marathon with sons and soon to be daughter-in-law. PET scan shows no signs of cancer, end palliative chemotherapy. Son Eric's wedding

June 2015- Ran Grandma's Marathon

July 2015- Rob Krar ultrarunning camp in Arizona. Pain starts to increase again.

August 2015- Cancer returns on a PET scan, re-start palliative chemotherapy

November 2015- End of palliative chemotherapy

December 2015- Start of hospice care

January 2016- Dave passes away at home

Made in the USA
Middletown, DE
28 January 2016